Son

of

Sassamansville

Son
of
Sassamansville

Leonard A. Swann, Jr.

authorHOUSE®

AuthorHouse™
1663 Liberty Drive
Bloomington, IN 47403
www.authorhouse.com
Phone: 1-800-839-8640

First published by AuthorHouse   08/19/2011

ISBN: 978-1-4634-4114-2 (sc)
ISBN: 978-1-4634-4113-5 (hc)
ISBN: 978-1-4634-4112-8 (ebk)

Library of Congress Control Number: 2011913150

Printed in the United States of America

To Gayle
My happiest moments come from
simply loving you.

CONTENTS

Introduction

There I was, late in the evening of May 1, 2011, in my study, proofreading my manuscript when Gayle, my wife, burst in with the news that Osama bin Laden had been killed by American forces in Pakistan. "God Bless America" rolled off my lips. My historian's mind plugged that date into my A List of memorable national events during my lifetime—December 7, 1941; June 6, 1944; August 6, 1945; November 22, 1963; and September 11, 2001.

I proudly reflected on being an American. I was thankful for my Swann heritage, my rural upbringing, my country values, my educational opportunities, my multiple business experiences, our children and grandchildren who would carry on the legacy, and, most of all, for my wonderful, complete life with Gayle.

As a trained historian recording my memoirs, I rejected Oscar Wilde's view that "History is mere gossip." Instead, I accepted Thomas Jefferson's opinion that "A morsel of genuine history is a thing so rare as to be always valuable."

As the oldest male Swann of my generation, I was even more aware of my responsibility to share my memories with the next generation. Pablo Picasso's advice was "only to put off until tomorrow what you are willing to die having left undone." It is with haste and humility that I tell my story.

Village Days

Sassamansville in 1938 was more Mark Twain than John Updike. Sassamansville was a small village about 50 miles west of Philadelphia, Pennsylvania; or to be more precise, it was on Hoffmansville Road, about one mile west of Route 663, which stretched between Pottstown and Pennsburg.

Founded in 1683 by German immigrants, the village was originally called Douglass. Its name was changed to Sassamansville in 1837 to honor Henry Sassaman, who donated the money to build a church at the west end of the village. That church was named the Union Church and was shared by Lutheran, Reformed and Mennonite congregations. The local Lutherans decided in 1895 to build their own church, a brick structure with a three-story steeple and bell tower, about 1/4—mile east, and called it St. Paul's Lutheran Church. These two churches with their cemeteries flanked the village.

Leonard Alexander Swann and Marie Ethel Swann, my parents, were living at my Uncle Joe's and Aunt Helen's house next to St. Paul's Church when I was born in 1938. At that time, Sassamansville consisted of roughly 30 houses and 120 inhabitants with family names of Schoenly, Yoder, Bauman, Erb, Updegrove, Renninger, Huber, Moyer, Tagert, Rothenberger, Kulp and Steltz (virtually all of Pennsylvania Dutch heritage) and a handful of small businesses: Erb's Country Store and Post Office, which was next to the Union Church; Bauman's Apple Butter and Cider Factory, which was founded in 1892; Shupe's Dress Sewing Workshop; a small cigar-making shop; Renninger's Barber Shop; a small Telephone Switchboard Center, staffed by one operator per shift; Schoenly's Auction Barn, where used items of every description were auctioned every Monday night and monochrome movies were shown on Friday and Saturday nights; plus Uncle Joe's J.M. Swann Trucking with its one box truck to haul bulk milk cans to the collection station of Supplee's Dairy in Schwenksville and a 3-1/2-ton dump truck with a snow plow attachment.

Sassamansville was a place where everyone knew everybody else and their business. "If you live here," Mrs. Erb at the Country Store often said, "you better make up your mind to keep your mouth shut. You learn more listening than talking."

My grandparents, Sidney and Lottie Swann, had moved from Charles County, Maryland, in 1920 to settle on a 45-acre truck farm located 1/2 mile to the northeast of the village. Grandpa had worked as Chief Gardener for the Department of Agriculture in Washington, D.C., but decided he needed his own farm to support his large family, which numbered nine boys at the time of the move and would grow to 10 boys shortly thereafter. (With a good portion of Irish Catholic blood coursing through their veins, my Grandparents had a total of 15 children with only one being a girl; sadly, four of the boys and the last born, the only daughter, died shortly after birth.)

The truck farm, run by Grandpa and staffed by his brood, provided both a source of food and sporadic income in the summer. For Grandpa and his brood, "summer" was never a verb. Vegetables grown on the truck farm included tomatoes, potatoes, sweet corn, peas, string beans, red beets and rhubarb; the fruit crops were cantaloupe and strawberries. There were also three cows for milk and a large hen house for eggs and chicken meat. Some of the extra crop harvest and eggs were sold to local grocery stores and hawked by Grandpa and a few of my Uncles going door to door in Pottstown.

While Grandpa was the tireless farmer working from dawn to dust, Grandma was the loyal farm wife handling the cooking, baking, canning to stockpile food for the winter months, and tackling the never-ending laundry. However, her most important role was that of family confessor—in a Catholic sense—listening to her boys' concerns and problems and offering her advice. Her favorite mantras were "You can do anything you want to do" and "There is always a better tomorrow."

Tidbits about life on the farm and my Uncles' accomplishments and escapades splattered on me during my formative years and embedded shards of a fundamental value system and a reservoir of positive energy in both my conscious and subconscious being.

Uncle Russell (born in 1902) escaped moving with my Grandparents to the truck farm by taking off for Manhattan to pursue his dreams of becoming an actor even though he had no formal training or experience as an amateur actor. Shortly after arriving in the city, at the age of 18, he stumbled upon a casting call for a production of Abie's Irish Rose and was hired to play the juvenile lead. Abie's Irish Rose had a successful run on Broadway and then continued touring the major cities, keeping Uncle Russell employed for five years. He later appeared as Abraham Levy in a production of Sunny at the London Hippodrome.

But Uncle Russell's second dream was to be an illusionist, a magician at center stage, at the focus of the audience's attention. His theater schedule permitted his studying under Howard Thurston, one of the most famous magicians of the era. When his theater job ended, Uncle Russell could find no openings for a magician on Vaudeville—movies had taken its audience—so he became a stock broker on Wall Street, where he said he "was so afraid of losing his job that he came in every day with a new trick for his boss." The 1929 Crash ended his career on Wall Street. He struggled to find work as a serious magician in small night clubs and hotel lounges; then he changed to a comedy magician. By 1934, he was receiving regular bookings as a comedy magician in the major hotel lounges and night clubs in New York and around the country.

"Russell Swann is probably the best comedy magician in the business today," wrote the senior editor of Night Clubs—Vaudeville, New York City's entertainment newspaper on July 12, 1941, "and sells standard tricks by mock seriousness, clowning, gagging (old and new), and kidding patrons. He works with cards, rabbit, egg, a 'cobra,' and rope."

The story of Uncle Russell's rise as a magician was told in the comic book, Pioneer Picture Stories, June 1942, under the byline "Six Startling True Success Stories Of Brain Muscle In Action." His story, intended as an inspiration for young boys, began: "Russell Swann, the Magic Man . . . was born a man who was to bring new life to a dying art."

With his motto, "Don't fool yourself, that's my business," Uncle Russell became a renowned magician, featured for 19 continuous weeks at the Empire Room at the Waldorf Astoria in New York City, a record for any act. He performed at the Savoy-Plaza, where he became practically a fixture. His magic dazzled audiences at New York's Copacabana, Latin Quarter, Rainbow Room at Rockefeller Center, plus the Coconut Grove in Los Angeles, the Mark Hopkins in San Francisco, and the Palmer House in Chicago. He also performed at the White House for Presidents Franklin D. Roosevelt and Harry Truman. In 1953, Uncle Russell gave a command performance before Queen Elizabeth II of England. He received national exposure with his appearances on the television shows of Jackie Gleason (he performed on two Gleason shows), Ed Sullivan, Milton Berle and Kate Smith, which I remember watching on our eight-inch round television screen.

Uncle Russell never forgot his parents or brothers. He religiously sent money back to the farm to help his parents and specifically so that each of his brothers, for the first time, could go to the dentist and also for each brother to purchase a new pair of shoes instead of walking around in hand-me-downs.

When he returned for the occasional visit, Uncle Russell came as a celebrity, wearing his fancy tailored New York suits; sporting a beautiful female stage assistant, who was always named "June" and hung faithfully on his arm; entertaining us by pulling coins, dollar bills (never Benjamins), playing cards, and rabbits from our ears. He shared first-hand stories and advice on surviving in the big world out there. I particularly remember his advice on hecklers—"Laugh with them. Always be kind to hecklers. Let them die on their own." Uncle Russell was living proof of Grandma's mantra: "You can do anything you want to do."

Uncle Preston (born in 1904) was a self-taught mechanical engineer who worked first at the Boyertown Burial Casket Company and later as a salesman for Pneumatic Tool Company. He lived for years on Long Island with his wife, Violet, and three daughters, Margaret, Madeline, and Helen. Subsequently divorced, remarried to Catherine and relocated to the suburbs of Philadelphia, he remained aloof to avoid any criticism of his ignoring the Catholic Church's prohibition against divorce.

Uncle Allen (born in 1907) lived defiantly outside the Swann mold and was the only adult son who refused to attend Mass. My only memories of him run back to 1941, when my parents were building their first house, a small wooden bungalow on Route 663, about one mile east of Sassamansville. Dad was digging out the basement and foundation footprint with a hand shovel; it was excruciating and slow.

One night, Uncle Allen broke into the Township's Road Maintenance Equipment Yard, stole a bulldozer, drove it several miles down Route 663 to Dad's lot, bulldozed out the basement area, abandoned the bulldozer down the highway near the Hickory Park Restaurant, and then sauntered in for breakfast. The Pennsylvania State Police followed the bulldozer's cleat tracks on the highway from the equipment yard to Dad's lot to Hickory Park and there interviewed a waitress to identify the culprit. When Uncle Allen learned the State Police had secured a warrant for his arrest, he bolted to California. I never saw him again.

Uncle Jim (born in 1910) became a professional photographer and began working in Manhattan, in the early 1940's, as the staff photographer at the Village Barn nightclub. His day job involved my Aunt Lou in owning and operating a small motel in Rahway, New Jersey. When their mid-life crisis hit, they sold everything and moved to Florida for the gypsy life in a large carnival that toured the United States. Uncle Jim owned the photography booth (three photographs on a six-inch strip for a quarter) and Aunt Lou had a concession trailer for French Fries and Italian-Ice Cones. They bought property on Route 663, about two miles north of the family farm, and returned there with their carnival trailer during breaks in their carnival schedule. Carny Jim's favorite line was that his new hobby was collecting portraits of Ulysses S. Grant and Benjamin Franklin.

Uncle Joe (born in 1912) was my closest uncle, from both a geographic and motivational standpoint. I spent my first years sharing his house and for the period of my life spent in my parent's house, Uncle Joe, Aunt Helen and their children, Charlotte and Michael, lived next door. He was a talented self-made man, starting at age 19, with one old truck and building J.M. Swann Trucking that ran milk trucks, dump trucks and, for over 20 years, the school buses for the entire township. His other business enterprises included a Real Estate Agency, Insurance Brokerage, Construction Inspection Service, and appointment as a Justice of the Peace. His business philosophy was, "When you rest, you rust."

From a personality perspective, Uncle Joe was closest to my Grandma. His assigned chores—helping her with the daily housework of peeling potatoes, washing dishes and scrubbing the floors—resulted in his assuming Grandma's humility and spirituality (for most of his adult life, he went to Mass everyday) and her philosophy "There is always a better tomorrow."

Uncle Sidney (born in 1914) carried the patriarch's complete name and the mantle as the slowest of the boys, never graduating from high school and always experiencing bad luck in most situations. Stories about him were legendary. He was a dedicated farm hand caring for the livestock but they kept tools away from him. "Give Sydney an anvil and he'll break it." And his brothers observed: "When Sidney separates the wheat from the chaff, he saves the chaff."

Or the family was sitting around the kitchen table and there was one chicken leg remaining on the dinner platter. My Grandma asked each boy if they wanted the last leg and each politely answered "No, Ma'am." Suddenly the electric lights flickered. When the lights stabilized, Uncle Sydney had six fork wounds in his right hand which he had used to grab the chicken leg.

Another time my uncles went to Turkey Buzzard Hill, a local road house. While most hovered at the bar, Uncle Sydney went into the kitchen to flirt with the dishwasher. A fight broke out at the bar. Uncle Sydney rushed through the kitchen door to help his brothers but was immediately hit across the head with a beer bottle. He was taken home with a lump on his head and blood spatter all over him only to be berated and grounded by Grandpa.

In World War II, Uncle Sydney left his foundry job when drafted into the Navy. In boot camp, Uncle Sidney told the base barber that he wanted to keep his sideburns. "Hold out your hands," the barber replied. Uncle Sidney was assigned to be the tail gunner in a TBY-2 Seawolf Torpedo Bomber, the most vulnerable spot on the aircraft, and flew combat missions against the Japanese in the Pacific theater. Who would imagine being in the Navy, not at sea but spending his entire flight experience facing backwards in a TBY-2 Seawolf?

After the war, Uncle Sydney and Aunt Sarah, his wife, purchased a small house and land over the western hill from the family farm. It became known as "Sydney's Back 40." Uncle Sydney saw his brothers thriving by starting their own businesses, decided to start an equipment rental company on his "Back 40" and purchased a franchise with 12 small rototillers for rental. Perhaps suffering the Pygmalion Effect, he did not rent one machine, because there was no demand for walk-behind rototillers, hidden off the beaten track in the "Back 40," and offered for rental to a farming community where everyone had access to a family-owned tractor. The rototillers, which Uncle Sydney proudly pointed out were "lined up alphabetically by height," became rusty monuments to his failed dream.

What kept Uncle Sydney barely financially afloat was his regular job as a welder at Bethlehem Steel's fabricating plant at Pottstown. One day a steel beam fell and crushed his leg, forcing an amputation and dumping him into retirement. His small disability insurance was allocated to expand a costume business that Aunt Sarah initially had started to custom-make costumes for rental to cast members of the theater productions at the local high schools and civic opera groups and then recycled them as rental costumes for Halloween. Uncle Sydney purchased my Dad's first house, the bungalow on Route 663, and built a little costume shop next door. Uncle Sydney announced his long range plan: "Go to bed at night and get up in the morning." He closed out his life, sitting in that shop among the thousands of costumes, watching Aunt Sarah sew, and hobbling to the Sassamansville Fire House for the Friday night poker games. Even there he had no luck in drawing the winning cards.

Uncle Jack (born in 1915) did well in high school, graduating as Salutatorian, then worked at the Boyertown Burial Casket Company and a State Liquor Store until he was accepted in 1938 in the Pennsylvania State Police, where he spent 35 years, retiring as a Captain. The words "stern" . . . "strict" . . . "integrity" . . . and "straight shooter"—both literally and figuratively—best describe him. His only distractions from his obsession with law enforcement were his devotion to Louise and Karen, respectively his wife and daughter, plus his hobbies of playing cards (Poker, Pinochle, and Canasta) and collecting United States coins. Uncle Jack was very close to my Dad and was my Godfather, who came many times to my rescue.

My Dad, Leonard (born in 1918), was considered by his brothers to be the most talented. While a more in-depth picture of him will be revealed throughout this memoir, his siblings were awed by his innate mechanical ability to diagnose the cause of engine problems by merely listening to their sound; his radio expertise, securing an Amateur Radio License W3KLB and building his own radio studio with a 1000-watt transmitter; his musical talents, playing the guitar and performing as the lead singer in a local western band with venues at amusement parks, fire houses and weddings; a pilot who flew both single and dual engine planes; and entrepreneur who turned driving a dump truck into a thriving heating oil company—all before he was 44 years old and with time out for four years in the United States Navy. Dad was another poster boy for Grandma's mantra "you can do anything you want to do."

Uncle Vernon (born in 1920) was nicknamed "Barney" by his brothers because his daily chore was mucking the cow barn. So it was ironic that upon his enlistment in early 1942 in the Army Air Forces, he immediately became one of the rural boy "shit kickers." He served as a navigator on the B-24 Liberator; flew 30 combat missions over Germany, including the bombing of Dresden; survived his B-24 being shot down over the North Sea and spent days in a raft before being rescued; and was awarded the Distinguished Flying Cross.

After the War, Uncle Vernon attended Villanova University for two years under the GI Bill but became bored with civilian living and re-enlisted in the Army Air Forces. There he gained a well-deserved accolade as the inventor of the portable tester that was used to test printed circuit-boards. His last billet, before retirement as a Chief Master Sergeant after 26 years of service, was in the elite emergency communications unit that would coordinate our military's response to an atomic bomb attack.

Now a civilian, Uncle Vernon returned with his wife Peggy to live near Uncle Jim's place, about two miles from the family farm. He joined the Computer Department of Burroughs Corporation.

Other than the fact that Uncle Vernon was a navigator and radioman in the Army Air Forces, no one in the family knew any details about his deployments during World War II—nothing, nada, nunca. It was only when my parents received a letter from a B-24 Bomb Group Association, requesting Uncle Vernon's current address to invite him to a reunion of crew members who had been shot down in combat, that he modestly revealed a few sketchy details.

Uncle Vernon's influences were very subtle but meaningful. From 1942 until my Grandparents died, he sent them $100 every month, which reinforced the importance of always helping and protecting your family. He was the first Swann ever to attend college, which proved that it was possible for a country boy to go to college. His secret advise to me was "smart muckers do not finish at the tail end," which was an oxymoronic revelation. But of equal importance was his gift to me of his leather flight jacket, which I wore as psychological armor during many stressful days at High School.

Uncle Dick (born in 1922) was nicknamed "Sugar" by his brothers, because as the youngest he got the most attention from Grandma. Reaching six feet and three inches in height, he was also the tallest. He graduated from High School in 1940, enlisted in the Marine Corps and was elevated to Master Sergeant in three years. He retired as a Warrant Officer after 20 years of duty, next worked in the Accounting Department of Westinghouse for 20 years, and retired again to start a third career as an ordained Deacon of the St. Joseph Roman Catholic Church in Odenton, Maryland, a position he fulfilled for the next 25 years.

Core values for Uncle Dick were "Semper Fi," a respect for the precision of numbers, a deep faith in the teachings of the Catholic Church and a devotion to his wife Doris and their three children, Carol, Sharon and Richard. Like his older brother Joe, Uncle Dick absorbed from Grandma her religiosity and her belief that "you can do anything you want to do."

Grandpa was the economic bedrock of the family. For this he needed a truck and finally bought an old Ford pickup. Unfortunately, he never really understood its mechanical intricacies. The contraption kicked him when he started it, spat oil in his face when he looked into its bowels, squealed when he mashed the brakes, and rumbled ominously when he shifted gears. Sometimes Grandpa would spit, squeal and rumble back. But he never won a single decision.

Frankly, Grandpa didn't drive the truck well at all. But he did drive it fast. When he went around curves, all the passengers' heads would duck into the truck cargo area. His sons had seen him nick fenders, slaughter chickens, and knock down full-grown trees; and they weren't taking any chances.

On Saturdays, Grandpa would load his Ford truck with produce and head to Pottstown for door-to-door hustling. A couple of his sons would accompany him and work their own hustles on parallel streets. One extraordinarily-hot Saturday, Leonard, dying of thirst, decided to sell ahead of the others. When Leonard felt he was far enough ahead, he ducked into the nearest drug store, confiscated a nickel from his receipts and bought a Coca-Cola. While he was drinking his coke, who should walk into the drug store but Grandpa, who also ordered a coke. When he noticed his son, he said with a smile, "It's a mighty hot day, isn't it?"

An economic mini-crisis occurred when the importation of cheap strawberries from Texas and California depressed the local market. Grandpa gathered the boys and pondered the problem. "We can," he said, "work hard in the hot sun, pick our strawberries, truck them to Pottstown and lose a lot of money. Or we can sit on the porch in the shade, drink a coke, tell family stories and lose a little money. What do you want to do?" They sat on the porch and raised their coke bottles to toast the strawberry invaders. That bottle of coke was their symbol of luxury. The only Christmas presents given to each son were one coke and one orange.

My Grandpa had a way of making every person know he was someone very special—not just one of the crowd, but as an individual with his own special reason for breathing. Grandpa would meet a gloomy looking person on the street and say, "Good morning." Then he would inquire about the health of that person's mother. When that person walked away from my Grandpa, there was a smile on his face. "You must respect each individual," Grandpa often said, "because if everyone thought the same way, they would have married your Grandma." Yes, Grandpa was a remarkable man, for it took a remarkable man to keep peace in a family of 10 boys.

But Grandma was the unquestioned matriarch. Her sons consulted her about their personal problems. Like a Catholic priest in the confessional, Grandma would shepherd each boy to the enclosed back porch of the farmhouse, listen to his problems, dispense her suggestions for resolution and dismiss him with a pontifical hug. This routine continued throughout their adult lives. Anticipated at Sunday gatherings at the farmhouse was Grandma's huddling with each adult son on the back porch for his private session; and the wives, squirming and stealing quizzical glances at each other, would nervously mouth the question: "What are they talking about?" Nevertheless, no wife publicly challenged it. The Swann boys would seek Grandma's confessional until the day she passed away.

The most important outsider, who was accepted unconditionally by the family, was Father Leo J. Letterhouse, the pastor of St. Philip Neri Roman Catholic Church in East Greenville and its tiny Visitation

Blessed Virgin Mary church at Green Lane, where the family attended mass. Father Letterhouse had been born in Bally, about 4 miles west of Sassamansville. Significantly, Bally was the site of America's first Catholic Church. Father Letterhouse was more than a local parish priest who officiated at mass and their baptisms, weddings and funerals. He was an educated man and thus their trusted source of medical information and legal advice; but most importantly, he was a dependable friend at every family crisis.

Did the 17-year old Marie Ethel Brey have any clue about what she was getting into when she married Leonard Swann in December 1937 in Elkton, Maryland? Born in 1920 in Pennsburg, Marie was the only daughter of William and Maggie Brey. Of Holland Dutch heritage, Grandpa Brey was a stoic man, very aloof, who worked as a bookkeeper at a local dress factory. His nonbusiness interests were playing pinochle at the Fire House, lounging in his big leather chair as he listened nonstop to the radio, attending services at the neighborhood St. Paul's Lutheran Church and walking everywhere, since he refused to drive an automobile. Grandpa Brey marching down Main Street, with his worn leather satchel, was a familiar sight in Pennsburg.

Grandma Brey was second-generation Holland Dutch; her mother came as an immigrant housekeeper for a family in Quakertown, Pennsylvania. Following in her mother's footsteps, Maggie Lizzie Kerr—called Lizzie by her family—graduated grade school only to begin working as a housekeeper, became pregnant with her first daughter Anna, married James Dewees, and moved without him to Pennsburg, where she found a job as a sewing machine operator in a dress factory. There she met a shy, middle-aged bookkeeper, fell in love with him, divorced the phantom James Dewees in June 1913 and married William Brey in July. From then on, she answered only to "Maggie." Their daughter, Marie Ethel, was born on November 29, 1920.

My Mother Marie would reveal very little about her childhood, other than to reminisce on how much she liked reading romance novels and how fascinated she was with "high—flutin' words." Bookkeeping and typing were her other favorite subjects. She also had a few lessons on the violin in high school. One night, she skipped a Pennsburg High School event to sneak with some classmates to a bowling alley. There she met Leonard Swann, began dating secretly (he was Catholic), became pregnant, left high school during her junior year for marriage, and gave birth to me on July 14, 1938. Although I was named after my Dad, I was not called "Len" or "Lenny" or "Junior" but "Sonny."

My parents started their married life in Sassamansville, staying in a second-floor bedroom at Uncle Joe's house. Uncle Joe generously covered their everyday living expenses. Dad drove the J.M. Swann dump truck. After winning a jackpot of $100 from a punch card at the Gilbertsville Fire House, Dad purchased a one-half-acre lot on Route 663, a little north of the Hoffmansville Road intersection leading west to Sassamansville. There, in 1941, Dad constructed a frame Cape Cod house, with four rooms and a bathroom. For the first time, I had my own real bed in the corner of the room behind the kitchen; in the other corner stood my parent's wooden desk with Mother's favorite book, <u>Webster's Dictionary</u>, which she consulted often for solving her crossword puzzles in the <u>Pottstown Mercury</u>, the daily newspaper.

Life was good. I was so happy and cheerful that my nickname "Sonny" could have been spelled "Sunny." My only chores were feeding the two family dogs that were tied to doghouses in the backyard, scooping their poop when ordered by Mother, taking the trash to the 55-gallon burn drum and carrying ashes from the coal furnace in the basement to the pile at the back of our property. After completing these chores, I was free to play Cowboys and Indians in the cornfields next door, catch tadpoles and frogs in a rivulet behind our lot, play with my green wooden jeep with red spools for soldiers, or reach for the sky on the rope swing that Dad had hung on the largest tree on our property line.

Suddenly my world became cloudy and gloomy. The Japanese Attack on Pearl Harbor on December 7, 1941, could not have been more devastating had the Japs bombed Sassamansville itself. Everyone was angry at the Japs and that was all you heard everywhere—at Erb's Country Store and Post Office, at the weigh station of the quarry where Dad loaded gravel in Uncle Joe's dump truck, and even after mass at the Catholic Church in Green Lane. To my four-year old ears: "Japs were bad . . . we must kick their butts . . . send the yellow guerrillas back to Hell."

Added to this cacophony was a sudden disgust with the Germans and the war in Europe. Adolph Hitler's maniacal rantings, the haughty racism of the Germans, the blitz attacks of the German army and the mass bombings of civilians were ratcheting up the local anger even more. In my confusion, I asked my Mother if our German-speaking neighbors were now our enemies. Mother quickly pointed out that they were not speaking German but were talking Pennsylvania Dutch and were good patriotic folks on our side.

My Uncles were swept away in the patriotic tide to defend our country. Uncle Russell became a Captain in the Army, touring the military bases with his magic act to boost the morale of the troops. Uncle Sidney served in the Navy as a tail gunner in a TBY-2 Seawolf Torpedo Bomber on combat missions in the Pacific theater. Uncle Vernon flew 30 bombing missions over Germany as a navigator on a B-24 Liberator. Uncle Dick enlisted in the Marine Corps. And Dad, my hero, was a radioman sailing the Pacific Ocean on a LST and saw action at the Battle of Iwo Jima.

Grandma Swann was particularly gloomy. She hung an American flag in the window on which she had stitched five large white stars to symbolize her five boys in the military. At church every Sunday, she lit five votive candles and knelt in prayer for what seemed like forever. And she found the hymns so sad, because no longer was my Dad's tenor voice leading the choir or closing the mass with "Amazing Grace."

I too was sad and lonely. I was Sonny without the sun. My Dad was deployed on a ship in the Pacific and could be killed at any moment. My Mother had given birth to my brother David on June 13, 1942, and seemed to be focusing all her attention on that cute sibling; his infectious smile captivated everyone—"Ah, isn't he so sweet." To make ends meet and cover the mortgage on our bungalow, Mother took a full-time job as a waitress at Hickory Park Restaurant, about a mile south of our house, at the intersection of Routes 663 and 73, and parked David and me in Sassamansville with an elderly woman she hired to babysit us, which was like being permanently grounded with no play time outside.

On the Saturday before Labor Day in 1944, my Mother said to me: "Do you remember that Grandma Swann is always preaching 'There is always a better tomorrow'? Well let's get you ready. We're going to J.C. Penney Department Store in Pottstown to buy you a new shirt and a pair of long pants, because on Tuesday you'll be starting your 'better tomorrow' at Hoffmansville School."

School Days

There I was, more Tom Sawyer then Holden Caulfield, beginning my first day at Hoffmansville School. Located on Hoffmansville Road, half-way between Route 663 on the east and Sassamansville on the west, the school house was a 1-1/2 story, red-brick building, with a bell tower over the front door and two outhouses about 50 feet to the south. As you entered the vestibule, there was a water bucket for drinking water carried from a neighbor's well and a storage area for our lunch bags on the right side; and a large coal-fired potbellied stove stood on the left. The front wall was covered with blackboards; and the teacher's desk was located front and center. Tacked above the blackboards was a lithograph of the Gilbert Stuart portrait of George Washington. There were about 26 wooden desks for the eight grades of mixed-age students.

The Swann family had a history at this rural Hoffmansville School. In the early 1920's, my Uncles Jim, Joe, Sidney, and Jack attended that school together making up 15 percent of the student body. Their teacher was Stanley Bauman, whose family owned the Bauman's Apple Butter and Cider Factory in Sassamansville. And in the late 1920's, Uncles Vernon and Dick plus my Dad were students there at the same time. Thus, a total of seven Swann boys received the first eight years of their formal education at Hoffmansville School; and as number eight, I carried on the Swann legacy.

A short, burly woman, Mrs. Weber, our teacher, epitomized that old country joke—"she was so fat that when they said haul ass, she had to make two trips." Or you stared at her and saw Abie cake and shoofly pie. After she stoked the fire in the potbellied stove, Mrs. Weber rang the bell in the tower to indicate school was in session. She grouped the kids by grade, about three to a grade, and assigned a wooden bench-desk to each one. She explained that she would teach us the three R's—readin', ritin' and 'rithmetic. There would be 15-minute sessions on each subject for each grade. When she was not talking to your grade, you were to stay at your desk, silently study and do your practice work. There would be two 15-minute recesses and a 30-minute lunch break. Then Mrs. Weber pulled a large hickory stick from under her desk and, waving it like a baton, broke into song. "School days, School days, dear old golden rule days. Readin' and ritin' and 'rithmetic, taught to the tune of the hickory stick." She warned us that she would tune her hickory stick on any lazy or rowdy student and by rowdy she meant talking without raising your hand, messing with the pigtails of the girl sitting in front of you, using your penknife to carve your initials in the desktop or—horror of all horrors—letting loose fart bombs.

Mrs. Weber was a dedicated but overwhelmed teacher. She labored on teaching us the alphabet, and then how to print letters, to write in cursive, to read the Dick and Jane textbooks—"See Spot Run"—to construct simple sentences with subject, verb and predicate; to conjugate the verb "be"—"I am firm . . . you are stubborn . . . he is pigheaded"—to memorize significant dates and events in American History now that our fathers and relatives were fighting a foreign war; to perform the simple math of addition, subtraction, multiplication and division. As Mrs. Weber taught the three R's, I learned by my three R's—rote, recitation, and retention. I repeated the multiplication tables so many times that I felt like an altar boy reciting the rosary.

Teaching 15-minute sessions of different levels of the three R's to eight different grades offered an advantage. In this open classroom, a caldron of chaos, if I listened closely, I could process and learn the entire curriculum of all eight grades. By the end of second grade, I felt confident that I had absorbed everything academic that Mrs. Weber had to offer.

But social advancement was another story. I found recess time very boring. What fun was it to run around the school building to play tag? How dumb was it to watch the girls skip rope? And who wanted to hang out at the stinking outhouse, see the older farm boys flash their tools and hear their bragging about the sixth-grade girl they had convinced to flash back her secrets.

Lunch time was especially boring. My Mother's idea of lunch was a sandwich of one slice of bologna on dry white bread and a scrawny apple. The sight of that bologna sandwich made me nauseous. So every day on my walk home from school, I took that bologna sandwich, still wrapped in wax paper, pretended it was a bomb blowing up Japs and tossed it into a culvert, about one block south of our house. Some days, I recited a takeoff of the Catholic prayer "Ashes to ashes, dust to dust" with my version, "Shit to shit, crap to crap." I secretly shook my head every morning as Mother prepared my lunch bag.

Then one winter day, the culvert overflowed, creating an icy hazard across Route 663. The Township Highway Crew responded to the emergency call to correct the condition and discovered that the culvert was clogged with hundreds of bologna sandwiches, wrapped in wax paper. After many hours working to remove the garbage, the Highway Crew retreated to Hickory Park Restaurant for coffee and told everyone what a mess they had discovered. Guess who was their waitress? Guess who got a lecture about the starving kids in China? Guess who said "I didn't know Chinese ate bologna"? Guess who met the stick from under the sink? Guess who ate Bauman's Pennsylvania Dutch Apple Butter sandwiches thereafter?

Memories of the second grade were pungent because I had developed an acute sense of smell. A slight moldy smell greeted me in the schoolhouse, sometimes overlapped with the smell of burning wood added to the coal in the potbellied stove, and then interrupted by the bad breath of the farm boys or the islands of stink from their fugitive release of gas. And outside, depending on the direction of the breeze, the accumulated odors drifted from the outhouses, the chicken coops across the road, the cow barn down the road, or the sweet, sugary fermentation with a hint of cinnamon from Bauman's Apple Butter Factory.

Other memories of my year in second grade included Dad's surprising me by picking me up at school on the day he was discharged from the Navy; my hanging out on Sundays with Dad at the Hickory Park stage where he was the sound engineer for the cowboy music shows; being allowed to fish by myself for sunfish, carp, catfish and big-mouth bass at Hickory Park creek; and Halloween Trick or Treating at Bauman's Apple Butter Factory and bobbing for floating apples in their cider vat.

That winter, I began my first business venture. I took a dollar in coins from my cigar box stash and bought four secondhand steel-traps to catch muskrats in the creek behind our house. Sold to Taylor's Fur Coat Factory in Quakertown, a muskrat pelt fetched 25 cents. My first trapped muskrat froze to death. My second trapped muskrat remained alive and launched a vicious attack at me but fortunately was restrained by the trap's anchor chain. I ran home in terror, quit the fur business and saw my investment go down the creek.

In the summer after third grade, Grandma Brey rewarded me with a surprise trip—actually my first trip on a tour bus and my first trip out of state. We took the Perkiomen Clipper, a chartered bus, with her Ladies Auxiliary from St. Paul's Lutheran Church to New York harbor and caught a tour boat up the Hudson River to Hyde Park, the home of Franklin D. Roosevelt. Grandma Brey and her friends sat in the chairs at the boat railing, facing out to the river. A motor boat with a few old men began running parallel to the tour boat. Grandma and the other old ladies hiked up their dresses a little and spread their legs. The old men pointed, whistled, shouted and edged their motor boat closer. The old ladies waved and laughed, waved and laughed. Standing behind them, I wondered if old flashers never quit but just shared their wares from chairs. And were the old men in the boat alumni of the Hoffmansville School?

Late that summer after third grade, with three years of seeing the older farm boys flash their tools in the outhouse and hearing their bragging about how good their girlfriends looked when naked, I wanted to check it out for myself. So one Sunday, my cousin Charlotte, who was two years older, and I were alone in the strawberry patch on the hill behind Grandpa's farm house. I approached her with my fly open and propositioned her: "I'll show you mine if you show me yours." Cousin Charlotte ran down the hill and tattled to our Mothers. When I finally sauntered to the front porch, my Mother grabbed me by the ear—luckily my ear—and screamed: "When we get home, I will show your butt my stick from under my sink, and your favorite red bike will be confiscated forever!"

My uncles, flashing saprophagous grins, reached a chuckling consensus on how to defuse the situation. They proclaimed in chorus: "Sonny's finally proved he's a Swann with true grit. He is carrying on the Swann tradition and now has earned the right to be called 'Junior'."

This experience taught me that I had to avoid the antics of the somber Mennonites, who rode around in their horse-drawn carriages, and the reclusive hillbillies of Berks County, who distilled moonshine in their backwoods. Specifically, stay away from your cousins and do not go to family functions to pick up girls. But other than that epiphany, I was really confused.

The rural pulse provided a plethora of priapic phenomenons: the tall, glass milk-bottles from Longacre's Dairy shaped like skinny bowling pins; the long-neck green Coke bottles; the long sugar cone with a hand-dipped round scoop of vanilla ice cream on top; a big ear of steaming buttered corn; a hotdog and bun; a Talarico's hoagie; the largest tractor—John Deere; the most powerful truck—a Mack with the big vertical exhaust pipes; the biggest car—Buick; the biggest shotgun—a 10—gauge double barrel; the longest fishing pole at Hickory Park creek; the most powerful baseball bat—the Louisville Slugger; the bell tower on the Hoffmansville schoolhouse; the tall steeple rising from St. Paul's Lutheran Church; the humongous silos attached to the barns; the periodic sightings of dogs, cats, pigs, cows and chickens doing the humping dance; the favorite carnival game—hurling a big softball to knock down a stack of longneck wooden bottles to win the cuddly teddy bear, costumed in a fluffy dress; the church charity bingo games played to win live hens but with a live rooster as the prize for the grand finale; the usual babysitter's trick of locking you in a room to listen to a static, crackling radio—"A fiery horse with the speed of light, a cloud of dust and a hearty 'Hi—Ho Silver!' . . . the Lone Ranger!"—while her boyfriend sneaks in for a quick "Hi-Ho Silver"; and the old Catholic altar boy joke about the lady parishioner, Mrs. Green, who always arrives late for Mass with her gaggle of kids, and sits in the front pew with her legs splayed. The priest leans over to the altar boy and whispers in Latin: "Est Nooky Green?" The altar boy replies: "No Padre, est black." I replayed in my mind my recent trip up the Hudson River except all the old ladies were Lutherans. Add to these whirling scenarios my Grandparents and my nine testosterone-charged Uncles and is it any surprise that I was a precocious but totally confused 9-year old?

The fact that I was an altar boy made it even more ironic. This pious altar boy, who responded in memorized rural Latin to Father Letterhouse's prayers in Latin at every Sunday Mass, who carried the incense for the blessing of the altar and who held the plate at Communion to protect against any fall of the holy Wafer—the body of Christ—this altar boy was now questioning "Est Nooky Green?"

Just before fifth grade was ready to start, the Montgomery County School Board decided to consolidate and relocate grades among the rural one-room schools. Hoffmansville School was designated to house Grades one through four, with students bussed in from the entire township. Grades five and six were to be bussed to the Perkiomenville School. So for fifth grade, for the first time I did not have to walk to school but would ride a yellow school bus, which was owned and driven by my Uncle Joe, to Perkiomenville School on the Hoffmansville Road, about two miles east of Route 663. Leaving Hoffmansville School meant that I would not be with my brother David when he started first grade there. Our educational paths would never cross.

Mrs. Miller was my new teacher. She was enthusiastic, energetic, and exciting. But for me it was more of the same. I easily made perfect scores on my math and spelling tests. So I was allowed to read any of the classics of American literature that I wanted. Moreover, she felt especially sorry for me because I had broken my right leg by falling from my red bicycle and was hobbling around on crutches.

The local farm boys, whom I sometimes called "yokels"—I was still socially challenged—began to pick on me. One day during recess the yokels had me backed against the outside wall and were threatening to kick my butt if I won the upcoming year-end Spelling Bee and advanced to represent our school at the County Spelling Bee. One of the farm boys wanted his sister to win. As I stood on one leg, terrified for my safety, swinging my left crutch defensively, my Dad just happened to drive by in his fuel oil truck and stopped to rescue me. He visited with Mrs. Miller to tell her that he had enough of this barnyard nonsense.

Already my advocate, Mrs. Miller arranged for me to take Advanced Standard Achievement Tests and be evaluated by a psychiatrist at the County School Board's central office at Norristown. The results confirmed that I was advanced enough to skip sixth grade and enter seventh grade at East Greenville High School, where I would be the youngest student in that grade.

Incidentally, the aggressive yokel's sister and I were the last two contestants remaining in our year-end Spelling Bee. I purposely blew my word so that she could win, because after all, I already had received psychological approbation from Mrs. Miller, had been fortuitously rescued by my hero Dad and was scheduled to be liberated to that exciting new world of High School. What could my correct spelling of the winning word "serendipity" add?

But any serendipitous moments in Seventh Grade were overshadowed by a family crisis. My Grandma Swann, who was diabetic, suffered insulin shock from gyrating levels of blood sugar and had to be hospitalized to stabilize her and to determine an adjusted insulin regime. Since my Grandpa was very distraught, it was decided that I should have a sleepover at the farm so that he would not be alone. Grandpa always slept in a small bed, next to a pot-bellied stove, in the front room adjacent to the kitchen. I went to sleep on a couch, about 20 feet away, in the next room. Suddenly, I woke up to a deadly silence without any of Grandpa's wheezing and snoring. He was not in bed or anywhere in the house. I then remembered that he rarely used the upstairs bathroom but preferred the outhouse. I ran down the path and found him unconscious, sprawled at the outhouse door. I ran inside, cranked the telephone to summon my parents. They rushed up, carried Grandpa inside to his bed, called the family doctor for an emergency house call, and alerted my nearby Uncles Joe and Sidney. Shortly thereafter on May 24, 1950, my Grandpa died at age 69 without regaining consciousness. I served as an Altar Boy at his Requiem Mass and cried as Father Letterhouse concluded: "The world will mourn over the loss of a good man, but the heavens will rejoice over the gain of a saint."

My parents were completing the move into our new brick house, about a block south of our bungalow. Grandma was moved from the farm into our old house. In daily rotations, Aunt Helen, Aunt Sarah and Mother took care of Grandma, while Uncle Joe, Uncle Sidney and Dad completed the night rotations.

While finding Grandpa at the outhouse was traumatic, my first four years at East Greenville High School were average. Although my final grades in the English, History, Math and Science classes were A's and B's, my grades in Latin were C's. Also, I complained often about how boring Gym and Shop were. My Mother was not pleased and ranted: "You can memorize your prayers in Latin but you can't progress beyond 'Gallia est omnis divisa in partes tres' . . . a dumb monkey can climb the ropes and earn an A in Gym Class . . . I can't believe that it took you one marking period in Shop to make a three-legged stool . . . God only knows how long it would take you for four legs . . . and it took you

23

another marking period to make a wooden box to hold newspapers!" Although I hadn't thought much about being a country lawyer, I mounted a defense, ingenious but not necessarily original. "But Mom," I rambled, "Latin is a language, dead as it could be, first it killed the Romans, now it's killing me . . . my gym shorts kept slipping down and when I grabbed for them, I fell from the rope . . . the screeching roar of the jigsaws and lathes hurt my eardrums." It didn't work. I couldn't Tom Sawyer her into cutting me a break. She still grounded me for a month and gave me extra chores of washing dishes and picking bugs and Japanese beetles from her rose bushes.

However, I did learn to play chess. As part of our lunch break, the students would congregate in the gym while records were played over the loud speakers. Some cliques buzzed with the latest gossip. Others "cut a rug" to the popular hits "Shake, Rattle and Roll" and "Muskrat Ramble" or "Out Behind the Barn." Usually huddled at the top of the bleachers with me were my classmates, Walter Meier, Ray Schultz and George Parkerson. We played chess. We concentrated on developing tactics to penetrate the castle. We argued that a move had been completed because our opponent's hand no longer touched the chess piece, while shooting superior glances down at the annoying jitterbugs who simply ignored us nerds in the bleachers.

Certain events at High School were memorable. In one class, a farm boy mouthed off to Mr. Louis Pernik, our history teacher, declaring that he would not read the history textbook on the Civil War because history was a waste of time. Mr. Pernik, a former Marine, picked the farm boy up like a log, ran up the aisle with him like a battering ram, and drove his head into the blackboard, causing the blackboard to develop large fracture cracks. The farm boy was a little dizzy but he and the rest of our class were very respectful and well-prepared for every future history class. That cracked blackboard was a graphic reminder of the importance of history.

One day, I found my Mother's violin in the attic and decided to study violin in the Music Department, dreaming that I could someday play in the family jam sessions. I signed up for weekly violin lessons at High School and, as a coincidence was asked to join the Marching Band as the cymbals player (or percussionist, as I told my Mother). That banging spot was good, because the band played at all the East Greenville Indians football and basketball games, which meant that I had a free pass and excuse to attend these sporting events. The only negative was the nickname given to me by the drummers—"Goose."

"Oh! Say, can you see [bang], by the dawn's early light [bang], What so proudly we hail at the twilight's last gleaming [bang, bang]." Playing the cymbals put me at the most important school event: the Thanksgiving morning football game against the Boyertown High School Bears, our most detested rival. It started with a pep rally, where Father Letterhouse always gave the invocation that ended with "and Jesus, we pray, that the Indians scalp the Bears." How funny was it that this predominantly Lutheran community was so happy for a Catholic prayer for the East Greenville Indians? "O'er the land of the free and the home of the brave [bang, bang, bang]." Goose had banged it again.

Playing the violin was a different story. I didn't have the musical talent or creative discipline of my Dad. My fingers became sore from pressing the notes on the strings. My eyes teared up from the resin dust released by the bow. My ears contracted like sphincters when I screeched a wrong note. About the only song that I perfected was "Twinkle, Twinkle, Little Star." Then my Mother became seriously ill and was rushed to Pottstown Memorial Center for emergency surgery. Being a good Catholic, I lit a votive light for her recovery and promised to make a sacrifice to thank God for looking after her. When my Mother recovered, she was surprised that I had given up playing the violin to fulfill my promise to God. It was perhaps the only time that I outmaneuvered her. I often wondered if God were so omnipotent, why did he allow me to get away with it, unless he also had enough of "Twinkle, Twinkle, Little Star."

The musical legacy that I could not live up to was reinforced most Sunday afternoons at our new brick house, down the street from our first bungalow. Various Uncles and their families gathered in our new basement, which was designed as a music room with an upright piano. All were self-taught musicians. Dad played guitar. Uncle Jack struggled with the bass guitar. Uncle Vernon, the fiddle. Uncle Joe, the harmonica. Uncle Sidney, the metal spoons. Aunt Sarah, the upright piano. Their country-western repertoire included Gene Autry's classic, "You Are My Sunshine." Dad sang the lead in "That Little Boy of Mine," which was my favorite. When they started "She'll Be Coming Around The Mountain," my Dad would yell, "Jack, Jack we're playing this one in the key of C." Or he would suddenly stop playing and say, "Come on Joe, you're off key and behind time."

Aunt Helen, with her Polish heritage, often begged a neighbor to bring his accordion, or "squeeze box" in the rural lingo, and play polkas for group singing. Most popular was the "She's Too Fat" polka—"I don't want her, you can have her, she's too fat for me. She's too fat. She's too fat. She's too fat for me." Or "The Beer Barrel Polka"—"Roll out the barrel, and we'll have a barrel of fun."

Near the end of the session, my Mother would serve slices of Talarico's hoagies, sliced very thin so everyone would have some food. Mother's phobia was that she would not have enough food for everyone and then be embarrassed. For the finale, the group would listen to Aunt Helen, the family soprano and a vocalist in our Church Choir, sing "Ave Maria," accompanied by Aunt Sarah on the piano. "Ave Maria" was my Mother's favorite hymn. The entire group would end with "Amazing Grace," which for a devout Catholic family was somewhat ironic, since that hymn had been written in 1773 by John Newton, an Anglican Minister; he had been Captain of a slave ship and stopped trading slaves to become a minister, not a priest.

Another distraction from academics was my involvement in the Boy Scouts of America. I had joined the Sassamansville Troop, under Scout Master Leroy Steltz, earned more than 20 Merit Badges, became an Eagle Scout, looked forward to the week-long camping trips at Camp Delmont, and beamed with pride when awarded the Order of the Arrow. I received an expert marksman award under the joint program with the American Rifle Association. But like Atticus Finch, I could not convince myself to use my 22-caliber rifle to shoot a live creature for sport or food. My efforts to be a good Boy Scout made me feel as if I were following the discipline that my Dad and Uncles had exhibited in their military service.

My chores in a growing family business were another distraction. Dad had a service station pump for regular gas at his truck garage. On the weekends, I sold retail gasoline by posting a sign along Route 663 offering it at 18 cents per gallon, a savings over the service station price of 19 cents. Our company still made a profit since we bought at wholesale. Dad split the profits with me. My other job was mounting car tires that we retailed. A sledge hammer, tire irons, rubber mallet and a chain valve-stem holder constituted my equipment. The secret was to insert the inner tube, pull out the valve stem and inflate it without catching your fingers or the inner tube between the steel rim and the expanding tire. Once a Buick wobbling with a flat tire, driven by a high-priced doctor from Pottstown, stopped for an emergency repair. Dad pulled me aside and whispered: "Diagnose it as a collapsed aerostatic perimeter and charge him double."

At the start of my Junior year in September 1953, East Greenville High School and Pennsburg High School merged to form Upper Perkiomen High School. My classes would continue at the old East Greenville location. But I was indifferent to the redrawn school organization and name change because my interest in girls was moving up several notches.

I took a fancy to Shirley Sames, who sat near me in English class. We socialized at lunch and she agreed to be my girlfriend. To show my commitment, I inked "SHIRLEY," in big letters, on the thumb of my baseball glove. I arranged to stay overnight with Grandma Brey in Pennsburg so that I could sneak out and take Shirley on my first real date—my first date ever—to the local movie theater. When I arrived at her house, her father quizzed me at length before she was allowed to walk with me to the movies. It was our first and only date, because her father was an obsessive Lutheran and would not permit his daughter to associate with a Catholic.

My flirty attention turned next to a popular cheerleader, Judy Horne, nicknamed "Judy-Ludy" to differentiate her from the other Judy in our class, Judy Lasley. Besides taking the same academic classes, Judy-Ludy and I served on Student Council and were cast members in our Junior Class play, One Mad Night. In this mystery farce, she played the character "Depression" and I was "John Alden," both part of a gang of lunatics who invaded the Cutter Mansion.

One day, Judy-Ludy invited me to walk her home to meet her parents. It was like a scene from One Mad Night. The set was their living room with a prominent portrait of Martin Luther on the back wall. Her parents entered stage left, stared at me, shook my hand, muttered only a curt "hello," and exited stage left, leaving Judy-Ludy and me alone. This was the real Cutter Mansion, eerily silent and spine-tingling spooky, with her wacky parents probably crouching on the other side of the wall, staring through a secret peephole and itching to pounce on me for any lecherous look, suggestive chatter or improper advance. I exited stage right as fast as my 15-year-old legs would carry me and never socialized outside of school with Judy-Ludy again.

Acting in <u>One Mad Night</u> started my thinking about what I wanted to do after High School. Did I want to be a professional actor like Uncle Russell and escape to New York? Did I want to build on my love of reading and words inherited from my Mother and become a professional writer of stage plays or author of romance novels? Did I want to become an entrepreneur and join Dad in his oil business? Or did I want to have a career in the military, like my Uncles, and perhaps command one of the new nuclear submarines?

Uncle Dick encouraged me to consider the United States Naval Academy. He pointed out that with five relatives who had served in World War II, with two uncles currently career military officers, with Uncle Jack in the Pennsylvania State Police, and with Uncle Joe's political acquaintances—particularly with United States Senator James H. Duff from Pennsylvania—there was a good chance of my being selected for an appointment to the Naval Academy. The thought of commanding a nuclear submarine, under Admiral Hyman Rickover, excited me so I wrote to Senator Duff and received a booklet of "Regulations Governing the Admission of Candidates." Page 11 specified that candidates "must be no less than 17 years of age . . . on July 1 of the calendar year in which they enter the Naval Academy." My birthday was July 14, which meant that I could not enter until one year after my graduating from High School.

Not one to be deterred, Uncle Dick pointed out a practical solution. Attend a military prep school for one year; and he knew just the right one, Valley Forge Military Academy at Wayne, Pennsylvania. So my parents scheduled a visit to Valley Forge Military Academy. The campus tour included witnessing a quarter bouncing from a perfectly-made bed in the dormitory; a walk-through the library with khaki-clad, stern students studying at sterile tables; and watching a parade of platoons of perfectly rigid cadets in full dress uniform, marching in cadence, with wooden rifles on their shoulders. All in all, I was not too excited with this preppy detour but if that's what it took to get into the Naval Academy, enroll me and give me a bouncy quarter.

But it was bucking not bouncing that had my attention. While I was still 15 years old, Dad began teaching me to drive an old stick-shift pickup truck on the dirt road running from Bruno Decker's farm, adjacent to our old bungalow, to the Hoffman's farm—"Start from stop . . . clutch . . . shift . . . gas pedal . . . clutch . . . shift . . . gas pedal." The pickup bucked and swerved, bucked and swerved. Once I bucked past the Deckers on their evening walk, blew my horn and continued to the turnaround at the Hoffman's farm. When the Deckers saw the pickup returning, they ran up a bank and hid behind a tree. Dad moved my practice drives to a local cemetery.

How exciting were my 16th birthday and my birthday present from my parents—a black, stick-shift 1949 Ford! My Driver's License! My own car! Now I was the man! For pointers on creating the new me, I secretly started reading the contraband <u>Playboy Magazine</u> in my closet after bedtime and researching what made Hugh Heffner so successful with women. I concluded it was his witty conversation and that shiny-white, slender, elliptical pipe he always waved to emphasize his points. I purchased a white pipe (which I never smoked), practiced my pipe gestures and looked forward to hanging out at the soda fountain after school.

On my first day of my Senior year at Upper Perkiomen, I drove my 1949 Ford and parked behind a green jeep. Out jumped Judy Lasley, suntanned and stunning in her red skirt. We walked together to our homeroom; as we chatted about our summer, I surreptitiously rubbed the white pipe in my pocket.

Although we had shared academic classes, my only previous involvement with Judy Lasley, who had moved into the area from New Jersey a few years earlier, had been as cast members in <u>One Mad Night</u>. Judy, wearing a regal white-velvet gown, had played "Lady Macbeth," a hilariously delusional Lady Macbeth who takes fragments of familiar Shakespeare quotations from various plays and delivers them as if they were from one play—"Romeo, Romeo, wherefore art thou" . . ."Out, Out, damn spot" . . ."Lay on, Macduff." Her role was better than my lame John Alden.

But now in our senior year, our paths were to intertwine. I was the Editor-in-Chief of the annual edition of <u>Walum Olum</u>, our school Yearbook; and Judy was the artist for its production. (The original name, "Walum Olum," traces back to the Lenni Lenape Indians, who, in about 1000 A. D., settled in the region now known as Eastern Pennsylvania. The first recorded history of the Lenni Lenape Indians was called "Walum Olum" and consisted of drawings on birch-bark planks.) Judy created the pen-and-ink sketches of Lenni Lenape Indian scenes for the inside covers and the chapter dividers.

Our Senior Class play, performed December 10 and 11, was Our Miss Brooks, a comedy with Judy playing "Miss Brooks" and I was "Hugo Longacre," the male lead. The plot revolved around the frustrations of Miss Brooks, an English teacher, in her struggle to produce a school play amid obstacles presented by an overbearing principal. The secondary story line was Miss Brooks' husband-hunting escapades and her stereotypical preconceptions about sports jocks, which she focused on Hugo, the head coach, and their ultimately falling in love. Miss Brooks' last line was "Curtains going up. [Turns and starts toward COACH] This is the beginning . . ."

And it was the beginning. Judy and I began going steady. We studied together. We met after school at the local soda fountain, where I salaciously waved my white pipe à la Hugh Heffner, pontificated on the topic of the day or entertained with my comic routine: "Go on a cigarette date, down 'Chesterfield' lane, behind 'Raleigh's' barn, where it's 'Cool,' spread your 'Wings,' let 'Pall Mall' your 'Dunhills,' give up your 'Old Gold' to 'Phillip Morris' and if you don't look like a 'Camel' in nine months, you had a 'Lucky Strike'." Or I would plow into my Sassamansville farmer pickup line: "I'm not a 'string bean' but an 'arugula' guy who'll 'turnip'; so 'lettuce' mash your 'sweet potato' and 'hot tomatoes' and then we 'cantaloupe' to 'rhubarb' behind the 'pumpkin'." Judy laughed and laughed.

Judy's opening line in her autobiographical paragraph in the Walum Olum was "Can be found with Len." Mine kicked off with "Interested in Judy." My favorite saying, reported in the student newsletter, the "Perk-o-Later," was Julius Caesar's "Veni, Vidi, Vici." Our Senior Class voted Judy the "most artistic" and me, "most likely to succeed." We started serious discussions about being together permanently after she graduated from her Art Studies at Edinboro State Teachers College and my becoming a Naval Officer after completing the Naval Academy. We were in love and saw no limits to our future together.

If April were the cruelest month for T.S. Eliot, May was the festive, flippant and frenetic month for the Seniors at Upper Perkiomen. Many chuckled about their "Last Will and Testament" in the Walum Olum: "Shirley Sames wills her pizza pie recipe to all Italians . . . Judy Horne wills her bugle to Mr. Neiman [our handsome Math teacher] . . . Judy

Lasley wills her jeep to anyone who can withstand cold weather . . . Leonard Swann leaves his diversified vocabulary to Daniel Webster." As Chairman of the Senior Prom Committee, I was scurrying around on last minute details. Some Seniors practiced the latest dance craze, "The Bunny Hop," featured on Philadelphia's WFIL-TV's Bob Horn's "Bandstand" in preparation for our Senior Prom—"Put your right foot forward, put your left foot out . . . Do the Bunny Hop . . . Hop . . . Hop . . . Hop." Others fantasized about slow dancing to "Out Behind the Barn" and their "getting lucky" afterwards. All salivated with anticipation of emancipation on Graduation Day.

But something was troubling Judy. She wrote me a weird letter, which included a 45-line poem that she had composed and entitled "Circles." Her letter ended: "Beyond the universe, bound by a circle and consisting of spheres, is the infinite into which no finite mind can penetrate. From this infinite realm, however, may come the line of vision, of faith dispelling chaos and offering to those who wish to see the beauty of art, of literature, religion—the beauty of life . . . Love, Judy." How weird! Our classmates were perfecting their "Bunny Hop" and she was rambling on about circles and the beauty of life.

Definitely something was troubling Judy. In art class she obsessively was molding and remolding, with green clay, multiple miniature sculptures of a squatting Buddha with a woman's head. Towards the end of the month she blurted out: "I'm pregnant . . . I don't want to have a baby . . . I don't want to miss art school . . . My parents will kill me." After my initial shock—"This can't be happening . . . I just got my driver's license last summer . . . Oh my God, Dad will take away my car . . . My parents will ground me forever"—I agreed with her that we really didn't need a baby. But what to do? We had heard rumors about a doctor who performed abortions in Easton, a city about 40 miles away and where nobody would know us. We skipped school and scurried to Easton to hunt that doctor down. We drove up and down the streets, checking at pharmacies for an address of the abortion doctor but found no one who knew his name. "I hate you." Judy started screaming, "I hate you! I hate you! I wish that I had never met you!"

So I dropped her off at her car and, in a panic, drove to see Uncle Jack at his State Police barracks in Quakertown. I confessed my predicament and pleaded for his help in finding an abortion doctor. "You are a Catholic," Uncle Jack began in his stern State Police voice, "you are a former Altar Boy. You know that abortion is murder and a mortal sin. Your only choice is to marry Judy, who you obviously love, and support your child. Go talk to your Dad and Judy's Dad. Work it out by doing the right thing."

I went directly home to talk to my parents. Their reaction was too calm, too rational, too consistent, which indicated that Uncle Jack had called to alert them and smooth the waters for me. Dad remarked that he could lecture me on life—"good life . . . low life . . . stupid life . . . wasted life . . . love life"—but instead he ruled that for an "honorable life," my only choices were to propose marriage to Judy and to be with her when she told her parents.

That visit with Judy's parents was the most frightening 15 minutes of my short life; wearing my Uncle Vernon's leather flight-jacket was my only protection. Her Father, John Paul Lasley, sat me in a wooden, straight-back chair, which unleashed visions of "Old Sparky" at the penitentiary. He kept glancing over my right shoulder at his gun rack on the back wall, where he had several 10-gauge double-barrel shotguns; and his silent lips kept mouthing: "I could kill you . . . I could kill you." Sitting next to her husband, Judy's Mother Helen, who was completely blind, was fiddling with gigantic knitting needles. She seemed to stare so intensely in my direction that I actually feared she would shoot her blank eyeballs at me. Instead, she screamed at Judy: "I knew you were no good! I knew it! I knew it!" Finally, after Judy's sobbing and my marriage proposal, her Father ruled that Judy was 18 years old and the decision was up to her . . . But! . . . But!

Shortly thereafter, on June 7, 1955, at 8 PM, Judy and I wore our caps and gowns to the Graduation Ceremony for the Class of 1955 at Upper Perkiomen High School. Separated by our alphabetically assigned seats, we witnessed our classmates being lauded, applauded, cheered, congratulated, praised, commended and admired by their families, only to face a deafening silence when our names were called and our diplomas were handed to us. Judy's parents did not bother to attend.

Next morning at 10 AM, standing outside the communion railing at the altar of St. Phillip Neri Roman Catholic Church—we had to stand outside the altar because Judy was not Catholic—we were married by Father Letterhouse, who had waived all the required formal Church announcements and waiting period. The ceremony took all of two minutes and was witnessed only by my parents, David, Uncle Jack and Aunt Louise.

At 11:30 AM, I checked into Sacred Heart Hospital in Allentown for a previously scheduled tonsillectomy. I begged the surgeon to give me local anesthesia because I feared that Judy's father might have influenced the surgeon's topographical intentions. Nor did it help, as I was being wheeled down to the operating room, to hear over the loud speaker: "Dr. Abelard . . . Dr. Abelard . . . please report to surgery."

A parochial, pessimistic and paranoid reality engulfed my return from the hospital. We were only teenagers; Judy was 18 and I was a month shy of 17, the youngest Swann to be married and the youngest Swann to become a father. But we were married, and a day at the hospital was our honeymoon. We had no place of our own, no privacy, and had to stay in a back room at Judy's parents' house at Zionsville, where I slept with one eye open, fearing that her father would grab his double-barrel shotgun. We had no dreams. Judy would not be studying art at Edinboro State Teachers College, nor would I be prepping at Valley Forge Military Academy until I became old enough for an appointment to the Naval Academy, which didn't accept married students in any case. We had no jobs. Judy couldn't work with her bouts of morning sickness. The thought of my working full-time at Dad's oil company was just too embarrassing, because it would require my figuratively tucking my tail between my legs and tolerating the risqué ribbings from the truck drivers. But what were my choices?

Then Dad sat me down. "Your survival," he said in his you-better-suck-it-up voice, "depends on two principles: Never let the bastards get you down and never, never let the S.O.B's know that you're hurting." He shifted to Grandma's "There is always a better tomorrow" and ended by pointing out that the first word in "family business" is "family."

Dad assigned me to work with a burner service mechanic to learn how to clean out furnaces and how to repair oil burners. It was a dirty, nasty, smelly job that often involved maneuvering in muddy, moldy crawl spaces or working in filthy basements. A set of coveralls and a pair of gloves made up my uniform. A bucket of solvent for cleaning the burner parts and an industrial vacuum for sucking up the dirty residue became my companions. A weekly paycheck confirmed that

I had survived another seven days but the gloomy days stretched out endlessly.

My gloom turned into blank despondency and then fleeting thoughts of committing suicide. But I couldn't kill myself, because I was a coward; plus my Catholic belief that suicide would mean eternal damnation was a powerful deterrent. And I kept hearing in my mind the voice of Grandma—"There is always a better tomorrow."

In late summer, my Dad and Uncle Jack decided that my purgatory should end and that I should be the first Swann out of high school to start college as a regular student. Uncle Jack remembered that he casually knew someone from some college in Allentown. A rabid coin collector, Uncle Jack had met some guy named Luther at coin swap events; and Uncle Jack had a rare nickel that this Luther guy wanted for his collection. It turned out that "this Luther guy" was Professor Luther Deck, who taught Mathematics at Muhlenberg College, and was a long-time friend of Harry Benfer, the Director of Admissions. A call was made; a nickel traded; an interview arranged; and an admission letter received. It is still frightening to realize that my life turned—not on a dime—but on a nickel.

Muhlenberg Days

There I was, neither Tom Sawyer nor Holden Caulfield, barely 17 years old in the fall of 1955; married with a wife expecting our baby in four months; having experienced a resurrection from creepy crawl spaces; wearing the mandatory cardinal-and-gray beanie, not a coonskin cap; listening to the hit song, "The Ballad of Davy Crockett," on my car radio; commuting in my 1949 Ford to my first day of classes at Muhlenberg College.

Founded in 1848, Muhlenberg College was a private, four-year liberal arts college with its all-male campus located at Allentown, Pennsylvania. The college was named after Henry Melchior Muhlenberg, who had emigrated from Germany to Philadelphia in 1742 and established the first Lutheran Church in Pennsylvania. (Coincidently, his son, Fredrick Augustus Conrad Muhlenberg was born in Trappe, a small village east of Sassamansville, represented Pennsylvania in the first United States Congress and served as the first Speaker of the House of Representatives, 1789—1791.) Muhlenberg College's strong identification with the Lutheran Church and the Egner-Hartzel Memorial Chapel as a cornerstone of the campus were not important to this Catholic country boy.

Aside from the simple joy of being in college, what really attracted me from day one was the imposing building in the center of the campus—the Library. I had never been in a building so beautiful, so mysterious and so inviting. When you entered the front door, you walked into a throbbing temple of information with four floors packed with thousands and thousands of books and archives of every major magazine. Browsing in the book stacks became my refuge from the routine of attending classes, jamming in required reading of reserved books at the Library, rushing home to be with Judy, working part-time at the oil company and studying late at night.

Muhlenberg's student population totaled about 850, with 250 Freshman. At my first Chemistry class, I was surprised to see Ray Schultz, my chess-playing pal from high school. Ray was also commuting to Muhlenberg; so we agreed to share the driving. It was good to have a commuting partner and a friend on campus.

Stellar moments of my Freshman year included my course in Elements of Statistics, taught by Professor Luther Deck. Whether he initially remembered me as the nickel-boy, I could not tell for certain. After our first homework assignment which involved calculations on a "parsec," Professor Deck asked each student, row by row, to define a "parsec." No one could define it until he came to me. "A parsec," I answered, "is a unit of measure of interstellar space equal to 3.26 light years or 19.2 trillion miles." A smile came across his face, perhaps in appreciation of what a nickel was worth. My final grade for the course was an A-plus; and Professor Deck allowed me to enroll in his Calculus course, without taking the prerequisite courses in Algebra and Trigonometry.

My only academic annoyance came from the Freshman Course in Writing. William Kinter, a mere Instructor in English, summoned me to discuss an assignment, my essay on steel. It was, as I recall, a sophomoric piece on steel—something like "The 'good' steel in spaceships and in skyscrapers will take you to the heavens; and 'bad' steel in guns and missiles will consign you to hell." Kinter accused me of plagiarism. "You have to be kidding," I blurted out in my defense. "If you think that I plagiarized for that dumb piece, prove it by showing me the stupid source." After that, he scrutinized my work with a magnifying glass and gave me one of the rare B grades that I received in college.

Of minor annoyance was the tradition of hazing Freshmen. The Student Handbook contained a section on Freshman Regulations: "All Freshmen must wear class hats and identification buttons which are to be worn visibly over the heart." Wearing the stupid cardinal-and-gray beanie and big name tags to highlight our Freshman status and surrendering to the Upper Classmen the right-of-ways at doors, sidewalks and halls were discriminatory—particularly when Freshmen were paying the same tuition. But I kept my mouth shut, because the hazing megillah was trivial when compared to working in crawl spaces and cleaning oil burners.

My real concern was Judy and our relationship. Reality was different than dreams in high school. Judy was uncomfortable with her pregnancy. She was miserable from the idle waiting with no privacy at her parents' house, which she characterized as "house arrest in Zionsville." She was depressed about missing college and delaying her training in Art. She continued to blame me for everything. But nature prevailed. On January 3, 1956, Debra Ann was born, healthy and adorable. I was relieved that it was not January 1, since the <u>Morning Call</u>, Allentown's daily newspaper, always ran a feature on the first babies born on New Year's Day.

The birth of their first grandchild caused Judy's parents to relax a little. Her father remodeled a large closet next to our make-shift bedroom into a small kitchen with a picnic table in it. Now we had almost 300 square feet of living space, could make our own meals and follow our own schedule.

Judy's spirits improved as her figure returned. She had dabbled with playing guitar and was happy when Dad gave her a vintage Gibson from his guitar collection to celebrate the birth of his first grandchild and showed her some techniques to improve her musical skills. Uncle Jack found her a part-time job as bus-girl for the dinner shift at a popular restaurant in Quakertown. It was not the job that was important to her but escaping the monotony of motherhood. While Judy worked in the evenings, I took care of Debby, with her crib parked next to my desk, and studied. Then Judy was accepted at Kutztown State Teachers College for the fall semester of 1956. We found a neighbor who would babysit Debby during the day. And the pieces of the jigsaw puzzle came together for Judy to start college.

Now the problem was money. We didn't have enough income to cover Judy's tuition added to my tuition and our living expenses. My part-time work at the oil company now involved driving a fuel oil truck to make emergency deliveries and making sales calls to secure new domestic fuel oil customers. After Judy's acceptance at Kutztown, her father decided to help us by giving me two new fuel oil accounts. John Paul Lasley was the Plant Manager of Sandura Company's manufacturing facility in Fullerton, a town adjacent to Allentown. Sandura manufactured rolls and rolls of sheet vinyl for covering floors. Its market was the entire East Coast of the United States. The manufacturing process was heat intensive and consumed seven to eight trailer loads (each 5000 gallons) of fuel oil each week. Judy's father would place all orders with our oil company, provided we met Sandura's current price. Moreover, Modern Transport Company, the common carrier trucking firm that hauled the finished vinyl products to Sandura's wholesale customers, would give us their diesel fuel business, about two trailer loads per week. I grabbed both accounts. My salary boost was enough to cover Judy's tuition at Kutztown and the cost of Debby's babysitter.

My experience at Muhlenberg became an intellectual nirvana. My professors were outstanding and stimulated my intellectual curiosity beyond my wildest imagination. Professor Harold Stenger, the Chairman of the English Department, with "Prince Hal" as his nickname, taught a full-year's course on William Shakespeare – the comedies, tragedies and historical plays with the noteworthy characters and their unforgettable quotations, which stacked up in my memory: "All the world's a stage, and all the men and women merely players" by Jaques in As You Like It; "The course of true love never did run smooth" by Lysander in A Midsummer Night's Dream; "Frailty, thy name is woman!" by Hamlet in Hamlet; "A horse, a horse! My kingdom for a horse!" by King Richard in Richard the Third; "The first thing we do, let's kill all the lawyers." by Dick in Henry the Sixth, Part 2; "But soft, what light through yonder window breaks?" by Romeo in Romeo and Juliet; "Lord, what fools these mortals be!" by Puck in A Midsummer Night's Dream; "Neither a borrower nor a lender be" by Polonius in Hamlet; "O Romeo, Romeo, wherefore art thou Romeo" by Juliet in Romeo and Juliet; "To be or not to be that is the question" by Hamlet in Hamlet. More quotations rolled off my tongue but as Polonius said in Hamlet, "brevity is the soul of wit." My final exam grade was the highest in the class; and Professor Stenger wrote on it, "An excellent job, well-conceived and well written."

Under Professor Stenger, I also studied the English Romantic Poets—William Wordsworth, Samuel Taylor Coleridge, Lord Bryon, Percy Bysshe Shelley and John Keats. On my final exam, Professor Stenger wrote: "A consistently excellent performance. Your comments are well organized and significant." My studies of Victorian Poets—Alfred Lord Tennyson, Robert Browning and Matthew Arnold—codified for me the world of Victorian values: faith, discipline, responsibility, stability, thrift and social cohesion. I scored a 97 on the final exam, the highest grade in the class, with Professor Stenger's comment, "a thorough job."

In Introduction to Economics, taught by Assistant Professor Herbert Fraser, the microeconomics focused on supply and demand, the effect on output and prices, the law of diminishing returns, fixed and variable costs—all buzz words from Paul Samuelson's iconic textbook, Economics: An Introductory Analysis. I received an A for the first semester. Then Professor Fraser called me into his office and asked where I had studied economics previously, because I had a firm grasp of the concepts. I replied that my Dad in his small business had taught me all the practical aspects of these economic concepts and that my Muhlenberg class was merely adding the technical terminology to what I already knew. For instance, The Law of Supply and Demand was evident with the shortage of the new Firestone Town and Country snow tires. With the high demand for snow tires in the winter, we could sell every tire we received from the Firestone plant at premium prices. Or my Saturday sales of gasoline illustrated the Effect of Price on Demand. Professor Fraser advised me to take the most advanced Economics Courses, especially Economic Theory and Macroeconomics. Surprisingly, on his recommendation, the Economics Department hired me as Student Assistant to correct all quizzes of the Economics courses, with a student grant of $75 per semester to be applied against my tuition of $405 per semester. For the next six semesters, I was correcting quizzes for the Economics Department. None of my classmates knew what my job entailed.

Although my course schedule was heavy with Literature and Economics, I decided to major in History. My initial interest was stimulated by a course taught by Professor James Swain, Chairman of the History Department, on World History, using his three-volume magnum opus, A History of World Civilization, as our textbook. The amazing Professor Swain lectured in class after class, without referring once to any written notes. His enthusiasm sparked my belief that in studying history I could embrace all of my intellectual interests and become a "Renaissance Man."

My real passion became American History, taught by Professors Victor Johnson and John Reed. Into the broad historical scenario—Colonial America, the American Revolution, the Continental Congress, the Civil War, the Progressive Era, the two World Wars, and the Roosevelt

Era—could be woven my interest in economics, sociology and also the great American authors. Plus my secondary obsession with British literary giants supplied an overall philosophy for Western Culture. Professor Johnson encouraged viewing history as the comprehensive story of mankind and man's efforts to improve society while protecting the rights of the individual.

Life as a commuter student centered on attending lectures and reading the assigned books and articles from the Reserved Section in the Library during free periods. I had to absorb the information as efficiently as possible, which meant grasping the pertinent material in one read through, because time outside the parameters of my class schedule had to be spent working in the oil company to support my family or babysitting Debby at night and studying at home. Critical were the engrained habits from my early years at Hoffmansville School—apply the three R's of rote, recitation and retention, listen closely during all the classroom lectures—and a new discipline of recording accurate notes from the lectures and assigned reading materials. I kept a separate, bound notebook for each course.

Richard Truchses, a classmate who became a clinical psychologist, later issued his impression of me: "I was quite jealous of him. He was a very intense kind of guy, an excellent student. He got a great deal accomplished."

Muhlenberg College was a community. I was a commuter. There was no extra time for participation in any extracurricular activities on campus. There was no time for any of the 31 Social Clubs, the six Greek Fraternities, the eight Honorary Fraternities or attending sporting events of the 11 athletic teams, each called the "Mules." The only exceptions were my memberships that resulted from special invitations to join Omicron Delta Kappa, the National Leadership Honor Society; Phi Alpha Theta, the National Honorary History Society; and Phi Beta Kappa, America's oldest and most prestigious undergraduate Honors Society. I was president of Phi Alpha Theta in my senior year and represented our Kappa Chapter at a national convention at Colonial Williamsburg in Virginia, which was my first trip to Colonial Williamsburg. It was exciting to visit the historical buildings and roam the streets where Thomas Jefferson, Patrick Henry, George Washington and many of our Founding Fathers had walked, and sense the spirit of their vision that created our nation. And coincidentally, Phi Beta

Kappa had been founded in 1776 at the College of William and Mary in Williamsburg.

I did not drink so I had no drinking buddies. In fact, I was too young to be served alcohol. The few friends that I socialized with on campus included Ray Schultz, my commuting partner, who shared his interesting work in chemistry; Mahion Cleaver, another commuter, who had a photographic memory and could quote Shakespeare plays, line by line, after one reading; Russell Purnell from the Pottstown area, who later married my cousin Charlotte of strawberry hill fame; Walter Schuman, who shared my enthusiasm for history; and Michael Sanders, who had an iconoclastic approach to religious authority and later became a Sales Manager in our oil company.

Judy's commuting schedule and courses at Kutztown were just as demanding and hectic as mine. Our married life devolved into two strangers meeting at night, exhausted, distracted and indifferent to each other. We looked to become more than friends with benefits when we moved, in early 1957, to our very own apartment in Bally, a small town about four miles west of Sassamansville. My parents' doctor had retired to Florida but wanted to keep his Bally house and attached medical offices. My Dad negotiated a trade with the doctor, whereby we would renovate the old medical wing into an apartment. Then Judy, Debby and I would live there rent free, would guard the main house and mow the lawn. Finally, we had our own place, privacy and the possibility of rekindling the excitement in our partnership.

That spring, Judy became pregnant again. She could not attend her fall classes at Kutztown, which ended her college dream. Her funk descended again. "I hate you" became her standard greeting. "I never loved you," she confessed. "The only reason I picked you in high school was I judged you the most likely to succeed."

On January 19, 1958, another healthy daughter, Rachael, was born. After spending all night at the Allentown Hospital as Rachael was being delivered, I arrived late to take a final exam in Comparative Religion at Memorial Hall. Instead of Acing that course, my final grade was a miserly B-plus, the only grade lower than the great big beautiful A's that I received in my last six semesters of college. Later that grade in Comparative Religion became the haunting difference between graduating as Valedictorian or Salutatorian. But as Grandma

Brey declared, while gushing over baby Rachael and little Debby, "The only thing prettier than a rose is two roses."

I was working obsessively at college and in the oil company—so obsessively that, during summer break in 1958, Walter Schuman, my classmate, began bombarding me with invitations to bring my young family for a vacation week at his parents' shore house at Ocean City, New Jersey. In one invitation letter, Walter observed: "I know that you have hit another straight A average . . . Your work has been the best in the class in all five subjects I have with you." In another invitation, he said, "All the work you are doing this summer . . . how do you maintain your perseverance to continue in your studies . . . My brother has brought down the crib." After our vacation with him at Ocean City, Walter wrote, "Earning a living and keeping a family plus going to school carrying twenty-one hours is too much. Something or someone is going to be neglected—possibly your family or studies." Well, it was not my studies, since I made Dean's List every semester.

Only 20 years old, married with two daughters, ages 3 and a newborn, I really couldn't take time to complain. Reality replaced romance. Responsibility forced a maturity. Work and study overrode fun and socializing. The simple foundation laid by Hoffmansville School—listen, listen, listen in the classroom and do not be distracted by stupid games at recess—complimented Grandma Swann's mantra, "you can do anything you want to do." My correcting tests in the Economics Department, my working part-time in our oil company, and my sales boost from the Sandura business made the economic pressures containable. However, my lacuna was my growing insensitivity to Judy. Her life was bogged down with two young daughters. Her second bout with postpartum depression seemed to last forever. It overwhelmed her dreams of returning to college or teaching art. She sat waiting, wanting, wondering and whining as she picked sad melodies on her guitar. Most of the time, I neither noticed nor felt her pain, nor did I remember my Aldous Huxley—"Facts do not cease to exist because they are ignored."

Label it "egocentrism" or "hubris" or "obsession" but the "I" took over. I decided that I wanted a career in teaching American History. Professor Johnson encouraged my investigating graduate schools to prepare for teaching on the college level. I applied to a half dozen Universities and was offered a full four-year scholarship at Emory

University and a full tuition scholarship for the first year at Harvard University.

My Dad initially was disappointed that I was not coming back full-time into the family business. I promised him that I could continue to handle sales to our industrial accounts over the telephone and that I would return during Christmas break and the summer months to negotiate the renewal of the contracts. "You should take," Dad finally conceded, "the offer from Harvard. You are the first Swann to graduate from college. You will be the first person in the Swann family to attend Harvard. In fact, you will be the first person from Sassamansville to go to Harvard. That's an honor. You must go to Harvard."

On June 7, 1959, exactly four years to the day after my graduation from Upper Perkiomen High School, I graduated along with my 181 classmates from Muhlenberg College. I graduated Salutatorian and Summa Cum Laude and also received the Luther J. Deck Honor Prize (that nickel was still earning interest), the Phi Alpha Theta Prize and the Daughters of the American Revolution Prize. But this time I was being lauded, applauded, cheered, congratulated, praised, commended and admired by my family and friends. As I was handed my diploma, I thought of Grandma Swann's promising "There is always a better tomorrow." And I knew where to look—Cambridge, Massachusetts.

Harvard Days

There I was, more L. Frank Baum than Jack Kerouac, driving a gift from my parents, a 1955 green-and-white Pontiac hardtop, with Judy, Debby, Rachael, teddy bears, blankets, guitar and suitcases, on the road to graduate school at Harvard University. Like the Pioneer spacecraft that blasted off in 1959, I was heading to intellectual heaven.

The summer months of 1959 had been hectic. It had started with the excruciating fitting of metal braces on my front teeth. My image became a 130-pound nerd, sporting a flattop and a painful metallic wince. Added to my business responsibility of renewing sales contracts for our oil company were auditing Introductory Spanish at Ursinius College in Collegeville to prepare for the language requirement of the graduate program and searching over the phone for an apartment near the university.

We rented a two-bedroom unit on the second floor at the Harvard Botanic Garden Apartments on Fernald Drive, about seven blocks west of Harvard Yard. It was a complex owned by Harvard and designed for married students. Judy's father moved our furniture there, including our picnic table for the kitchen.

Founded in 1636, only 16 years after the settlement at Plymouth, Harvard College was the oldest college in the United States. Named after its first benefactor, John Harvard, a minister who donated his library, it evolved into Harvard University, comprised of eleven Colleges and Graduate Schools that occupied 142 buildings on 4,979 acres along the Charles River in Cambridge. Everywhere the word "Veritas" leaped from the Harvard University shields.

My classes in the Graduate School of Arts and Sciences were conducted in Harvard Yard, dominated by The Harry Elkins Widener Memorial Library. Compared to my excitement at the Muhlenberg College Library, I found it paradisiacal to climb the majestic steps into

Widener Library, to roam the book stacks with its millions and millions of books, and to study at the vintage desks located in the stacks.

At the orientation meeting at Sanders Theatre on September 24, an Assistant Dean addressed us: "Welcome to Graduate School. Look to the person on your left. Look to the one on your right. One of you will not be here at the end of this academic year." Ted Sloan sat to my left but I didn't catch the name of the person on the right. That challenge not only contributed to my paranoia about fellow students, but also started my habit of averaging 11 hours of class and study time per day and justified my sleeping on the floor for an average of four hours a night so that I would not oversleep.

In a History Department bursting with nationally acclaimed professors, two mesmerized me in the first year: Oscar Handlin and Arthur M. Schlesinger, Jr., both holders of the Pulitzer Prize in History—Handlin for his book The Uprooted in 1952 and Schlesinger at age 28 for The Age of Jackson in 1946.

Professor Oscar Handlin, who was usually seen in Widener Library with Mary Flug Handlin, his wife and writing partner, presented an evolving interpretation of American economic history. His books alone were sufficient for the entire course, starting with Commonwealth, a history of Massachusetts, 1774-1861, that traced the shift from a commonwealth concept to "laissez faire," from the state to the individual making economic decisions; and then to Boston Immigrants, 1790-1865 and Race and Nationality in American Life in which his central premise was that discrimination resulted from inferior economic status, not from racial origins.

Professor Arthur M. Schlesinger, Jr., who had already published two volumes of The Age of Roosevelt, taught the course in American Intellectual History and a graduate seminar on Recent American History. I enrolled in both. The auditorium was crowded as he delivered spell-binding lectures on the influences on the American mind—Puritanism, Jeffersonian rational liberalism, Hamiltonian conservatism, Southern racial aristocracy, New England transcendentalism and frontier individualism, to name a few. I studied ferociously and received an A-minus.

For his Seminar on Recent American History, I researched the origin and effect of the Senate Committee, chaired by Senator Gerald P. Nye from North Dakota, from 1934-1936, that investigated the relationship of munitions makers, armament manufacturers and bankers on fomenting international crises and wars to generate profits; on the ineptness of President Woodrow Wilson in failing to keep the United States out of World War I; and the effect of the Nye Committee hearings on the pacifist and isolationist movement in the late 1930's. The paper was entitled "Senator Nye, the Nye Committee and Its Impact." My grade was a B, the only B that I ever received in a history course at Muhlenberg or Harvard. "This paper shows," Schlesinger wrote in his critique, "evidence of hard work and of some thought; but the presentation is lamentably, careless and slipshod. The writing is often loose and repetitious, and sometimes imprecise . . . your research seems thorough, and most of your analysis is convincing."

Having been slapped down by a Pulitzer Prize author, I became even more serious about a rigorous lecture, reading and study schedule. But I was often interrupted because I had become a family celebrity, confidant and confessor, inundated with visitors, phone calls and letters.

In October, Judy's Father, Mother and younger brother Paul arrived to visit Harvard and the Lexington—Concord Battlefield of Revolutionary War fame for "the shot heard around the world." They also brought a black English bicycle that my Mother insisted was necessary for my daily travel to class and Widener Library.

Also in October, Dad asked me to track down Charles Walsh, a manager of the Atlantic Refining Company, who was attending a three-month program at the Harvard Business School. Walsh was an executive in marketing at Atlantic, our prime petroleum supplier. We had several goodwill dinners together.

In November, Dad, David and Father Letterhouse flew in early one Friday morning. They toured Harvard Yard, snapped the obligatory photographs in front of the statue of John Harvard, dined at Jimmy's Harborside Restaurant in Boston, stayed at the Commander Hotel across the Common from Harvard Yard, and followed the Harvard Marching Band to the stadium for the Harvard-Princeton football game on Saturday. All found it amazing that Harvard had the tradition of welcoming alumni band members to march with the current student band and to perform without practice at the half-time show. "Old Harvard trumpet players never die," Father Letterhouse observed, "they just blow away." They caught a late flight home so that Father Letterhouse could cover his Sunday Mass.

Then in February 1960, Mother visited for a week and attended every lecture with me. She was surprised at the number of students, a combination of undergraduates and graduates that averaged about 200 at each lecture, a number greater than my graduating class in college. Mother enjoyed the lectures by Oscar Handlin on American economic history. She was already a fan of Arthur Schlesinger, Jr., because she liked his books on Franklin D. Roosevelt and she respected his work on the Democratic Advisory Committee and as a speechwriter for Senator John F. Kennedy, her Catholic hero.

One night, we took Mother to the Shubert Theatre in Boston to see the musical West Side Story. The next morning we heard her singing in the shower—"I feel pretty, oh so pretty."

Mother surprised me with a gift of two books that she had read, Allen Ginsburg's poem Howl and Jack Kerouac's On the Road. She proudly announced that Aunt Helen and she had tickets to attend a poetry reading by Fernal Getty at Muhlenberg College. Getty would be reading from his new book Love and Death. What was happening? Was Mother going over to the dark side with the Beatniks? She confessed that she was tired of the hassle associated with keeping the books for the family business and fantasized about the freedom of the Beatnik culture—or as she said, "the only rebellion around"—and reveled in the Beatnik word play, which was an uncharacteristic diversion from her crossword puzzles and Daniel Webster.

Inevitably, the nightly conversation turned to David, as the many phone calls and weekly letters from my parents usually did. David was goofing off at St. Pius X High School, had two failure notices in Trigonometry and French, and might not graduate. David was risking his life and banging up his car by drag racing on country roads. Three of David's friends had been arrested while burglarizing a service station in Limerick; and one had been wounded by the owner of that service station. Then, the leader of the burglars was discovered to be running an organized Teenage Gambling Parlor and taking a house cut from stakes as high as $100 per poker game, which made it illegal. Several days later, Dad found a loaded revolver in the glove compartment of David's car and worried that David might have been planning to join the gambling ring. Dad grounded David. David threatened to run away and enlist in the Navy. "Dave has been a problem and still is," wrote Mother, "he doesn't seem to care . . . When I talk about him trying to copy after Uncle Allen he just sits and laughs and tells me I'm a big joke." Both my parents asked me to write him a brotherly "straighten up" letter to which David replied, "As usual I flubbed." And in another letter David claimed it was all my fault that our parents had "no regard" for him, because "he doesn't measure up to my standards."

Grandma Swann, after months in a nursing home, died on May 9, 1960. As her Boyertown Casket lowered into the ground next to Grandpa and Father Letterhouse delivered her benediction, her voice was the only sound I heard—"You can do anything you want to do."

Weekly phone calls and letters covered the exasperating problems of growing a business, ranging from fixing equipment breakdowns and driver no-shows during snowy weather to chronic shortages of working capital. Throughout 1960, the pressure exploded. The weekly orders for industrial fuel totaled about 70 trailer loads. Without any notice, Pruitt Oil Company, one of our major suppliers of heavy oil, cut off the company credit of $100,000 and would only reopen it if Dad sold them 51% of the company. Dad managed to cobble together some bank credit and coupled with a loan from Uncle Joe, was limping along. Then, Texaco Refining Company bought Pruitt and reopened our company credit.

Next, the increased orders taxed our ten-men tractor-trailer driving force. Mother wrote that "Dutchman aren't happy unless they're complaining." However three of the drivers petitioned the Teamsters Union for representation. As replacement drivers were found, Dad fired the malcontents when they had minor accidents or cheated on their time cards. This resulted in an investigation by the National Labor Relations Board of the allegation that the three drivers had been fired not for cause but for their union activity. After much negative publicity generated by the NLRB investigation and rebuttal techographs to suggest that the drivers had cheated on their time cards, the NLRB dropped the case.

With all the distractions and academic demands, something had to slip. After her visit, Mother wrote: "Your reading schedule always amazes me and I often wonder how you find time to eat and do the routine things of married life." I simply had very little free time for Judy and my daughters. Judy felt like a scholastic widow with her days occupied by caring for Debby and Rachael. Sadly, Debby suffered a major skin infection, had to be isolated for weeks and could not attend her pre-kindergarten class. Then Judy slipped and fell on the ice, damaged her coccyx and had back discomfort for months. Next our car was stolen. It took several weeks until the police found it.

At nights when I could babysit and study, Judy was free to join the other Harvard wives in bridge games, to take private guitar lessons, to play jam sessions with fellow guitarists whom she met through her guitar teacher, to read Beatnik books and to attend Beatnik poetry readings at the Folk Clubs. ("If your Mother can go to Beatnik poetry readings, so can I!") She also became a shopaholic and frequented Filene's basement in Boston for bargains from the "Slightly Imperfect" racks. And my habit of sleeping only four hours a night, often on the floor next to our bed, did not help our relationship.

With the never ending distractions and madness in my daily schedule, it was a miracle that I earned all A's and only the one infamous B from Schlesinger, passed my French exam and received a Master of Arts degree in nine months.

That summer, we moved back temporarily to an apartment that Judy's Father had constructed over his garage so that Judy and the girls could spend vacation time with her parents.

My concentration focused on auditing a summer class in Spanish at Lehigh University in Bethlehem to prep for my second foreign language requirement, which I had to pass in early October to continue in the Doctor of Philosophy (Ph. D.) program. There was also additional pressure for increasing our firm's industrial oil sales and thus my income, because Harvard had not awarded me a tuition grant for the next academic year. I made a determined effort to lure Mike Sanders, my college classmate, to leave his position at First National City Bank on Park Avenue, New York City. Mike finally agreed that, after completing his duty requirement in the Air National Guard in September, he would join us as Sales Manager.

Another pressing task was to help Dad in planning the reorganization of the oil business from a sole proprietorship to a corporate entity that would limit his personal liability and made it easier to prepare audited financial statements that were necessary to secure Lines of Credit from the banks. Mike Sanders had recommended it as the way to avoid the cash flow problems of previous years. So a plan was developed to set up three "C" Corporations—Swann Oil, Inc. for marketing, Swann Rentals, Inc. for ownership of the truck fleet, and Swann Realty, Inc. for holding all the real estate.

The resolutions for my other concerns were falling into place. David was starting college at John Carrol University in Cleveland, Ohio. Debby was accepted for kindergarten class at Leslie-Ellis School, about three blocks from our Cambridge apartment. John Kennedy was the Democratic nominee for President. When watching the convention on television, I saw Arthur Schlesinger, Jr., with his trademark bow tie, hobnobbing with the Utah delegation during the casting of the critical ballot. Later, I recognized some Schlesinger rhetoric in Kennedy's "New Frontier" speech.

It was with pose, purpose and slight paranoia that I departed with Judy and our daughters for Cambridge. In early October, I passed my Spanish exam, which completed the requirement for the two foreign languages. I was enrolled in the four courses taught by the four distinguished professors who would constitute the committee for my oral examination in my four chosen fields required to receive a Doctor of Philosophy (Ph.D.) in history, namely—Giles Constable for Economic and Social History of Western and Central Europe, Middle Ages to 1500; Bernard Bailyn for American History to 1789; Frank Freidel for American History since 1789; and Robert Albion for Oceanic History since 1763.

Assistant Professor Giles Constable was so medieval that you expected to hear Benedictine monks chanting is his class room. He brought Mohammed, Charlemagne, St. Dominic and St. Francis to life and interwove the crusades and the Magna Carta into the economic and social changes in Europe.

Professor Bernard Bailyn was already on my radar because I had read his book, The New England Merchants in the Seventeenth Century, at Muhlenberg. His course in American Colonial history emphasized that at the core of the American experience and indispensable for the American Revolution was the conviction that power is evil and must be controlled by a Bill of Rights and the separation and balancing of authority in government.

Frank Freidel, the Charles Warren Professor of American History, was already an icon for his three definitive volumes of Franklin D. Roosevelt biography—The Apprenticeship, The Ordeal and The

51

Triumph. As in his writing, Freidel made history come alive in his lectures by emphasizing the actors, their personalities, ideals, goals and foibles. In a hall filled with a couple hundred students, his lectures were so compelling that I often found myself listening instead of taking notes and gazing at his flattop for a hirsute connection. He was committed to his students. In winter of 1961, a blizzard dropped about two feet of snow on Cambridge. Harvard had never cancelled classes in 325 years. As I trudged down Concord Avenue to reach Harvard Yard, Professor Freidel passed me on skis, having skied about seven miles from his home in Belmont to deliver his lecture.

Shining over most Naval and Maritime historians was the seminal book, The Influence of Sea Power Upon History, written by Alfred Thayer Mahan and published in 1880. While his Harvard colleague Samuel Eliot Morison in his 15-volume History of the United States Naval Operation in World War II emphasized the military aspect, Professor Robert Albion, Harvard's first professor of Oceanic History, concentrated on the importance of the merchant marine to commerce and the international economy. In collaboration with his wife, Jennie Barnes Pope, he wrote Square-Riggers on Schedule, The Rise of New York Port, 1815-1860, and Sea Lanes in Wartime, The American Experience, 1775-1945. In his course – which everyone called "Boats" – he lectured without referring to any written notes.

The only glitch in my second year at Harvard occurred when Professor Albion offered me a Graduate Assistant position, which would involve my correcting undergraduates' exams and helping with his research. That diversion of my time would have delayed my graduation since most Graduate Assistants spent about two years more for a total of six years to complete their degree. Regrettably, I had to turn it down because, as I explained to Professor Albion, I was already working a long-distance job to support my family and did not have an extra second to spare. I had to graduate under the four-year schedule. It was a diplomatic mistake that could come back to haunt me, since Professor Albion was Chairman of the committee for my oral examination; and he was the logical advisor for my planned thesis in Maritime History.

Diversions came from family visits. Dad, Uncle Joe and Father Letterhouse flew up to tour the Concord-Lexington Battlefield; to feast on a seven-course dinner at Locke-Ober's, a five star restaurant in Boston; to see the Harvard Gilbert and Sullivan Players production of <u>Pirates of Penzance</u> at the Loeb Drama Theatre; and to cheer at the Harvard-Yale football game, which Harvard lost. The Harvard Band's half-time show was a spoof on Yale's "Whiffenpoof" song. "You can't trust those Yalies," Father Letterhouse remarked, "because anyone who sings the Whiffenpoof song as his anthem, is a few pennies short of a nickel." I just couldn't get away from nickels.

My immediate family life drifted along as usual. Judy was polishing her guitar playing and folk singing. Debby and Rachael were practicing reciting the alphabet and drawing pictures next to my desk as I tackled the 136 books and 56 articles still on my reading list. On the way to my day-time desk in the stacks at Widener Library, I carried Debby on the handlebars of my bike to Leslie-Ellis School each day. Her teacher reported: "Debby is a delightful child with which to work."

My oral examination was scheduled for December 12, 1961, twenty years and 5 days after Pearl Harbor. Only my sadness came again on December 7 because on that day Father Letterhouse died suddenly, at the age of 74. I was shocked by his death and depressed that I could not attend his funeral. Then two days later, I learned that Mahlin Cleaver, my friend from Muhlenberg, had committed suicide. Mahlin had a photographic memory, which he had displayed often in our Shakespeare class. He had entered a graduate program in literature at Lehigh University, had begun losing his photographic memory, had erratic and crazy outbursts, had been institutionalized in an insane asylum and there had hung himself.

So it was with a heavy heart that I showed up for my oral examination before Professors Albion, Constable, Bailyn and Freidel. Fellow students had warned that if you answered "I don't know" you would automatically fail. Each professor had thirty minutes for his field. I only recalled a few tidbits of the two hours. Professor Constable asked me what I perceived to be a trick question about the commerce on the Byzantine trade route. I answered, "I don't know, because I had never read anything to clarify that aspect." Professor Bailyn questioned me on the movement of the British troops west of the York River in Virginia during the American Revolution. Professor Albion interrupted that the York River ran west to east so the British troops were south of the York River. The two argued for over 15 minutes, thus using up half of Professor Bailyn's time. When I was allowed to answer, I said

"Cornwallis and his troops were trapped either west or south of the York River, as the case might be."

When I left the room, I was convinced that I had failed. Professor Albion had promised to call me with my results. I rode my bike home in a daze, sat on the sofa like a zombie and waited for the telephone to ring. I sat there all night, staring at the phone and shivering with fear of failure. Finally at lunch time the next day, a registered letter arrived; its one sentence read: "I am happy to report that you passed the general examination for the Ph. D. in History." Later, when I bumped into Professor Albion at Widener Library, he said that he didn't phone me because he had sensed that I knew that I had passed!

We took an early Christmas Break and headed to Pennsylvania to celebrate. On the New Jersey turnpike, I drifted off the road and side swiped a pole with our Pontiac. Fortunately, no one was hurt. Dad decided a safer car was needed and gave me his 1959 Mercedes.

For the next 18 months, life at Harvard settled down to the graduate school three R's—researchin', readin' and ritin'—for my thesis on John Roach, with Professors Albion and Freidel as my thesis advisors. For Professor Albion's seminar in Oceanic History, I previously had written a paper "The Development of United States Steamship Transportation on Export Commerce to Brazil, 1865-1893." The key figure was John Roach, an Irish immigrant to the United States in 1832. Roach labored in an iron foundry and learned to cast the parts for steam engines; acquired ownership of a foundry to make steam engines for the Union Navy during the Civil War; built his own shipyard in Chester, Pennsylvania, to make iron vessels; acquired his own coal and iron mines for the raw materials; built vessels for operating his own steamship line between the U.S. and Brazil, thus being the first businessman in the United States to introduce the concept of vertical integration from raw material to manufacturing facilities to steamship operations. Roach went on to build the *Atlanta*, the *Boston*, the *Chicago*, and the *Dolphin*, the first steel ships in the United States Navy. No historian had investigated Roach's accomplishments as a Maritime Entrepreneur.

To tell Roach's story, I had to travel away from my family and track down any original documents in the Library of Congress in Washington, D.C.; the New Hampshire Historical Society in Concord, New Hampshire; the New York Historical Society in New York City; Rutherford B. Hayes Library in Fremont, Ohio; the Marine Historical

Association in Mystic, Connecticut; the Mariner's Museum in Newport News, Virginia; the Delaware County Historical Society in Media, Pennsylvania and Roach's descendants in Pennsylvania and Virginia.

The research for Roach's biography was demanding but exciting. It required the skills and determination of a detective, following one clue after another. It was gaining access to unpublished personal papers for first-hand information. Most exciting was finding Roach's living descendants—one in Media, Pennsylvania, about 40 miles from Sassamansville—and discovering unpublished family photographs of John Roach and his Chester shipyard, plus a rare letter believed to have been written by his hand and signed by him to suggest that he could read and write.

I was fortunate that the fellow on my left on orientation day, Ted Sloan, had become a friend and joined me in the surviving duo from the intimidated trio. Also, Ted was writing his thesis under Professor Albion on Benjamin Franklin Isherwood, a United States Navy engineer, who crossed paths with John Roach from his early steam engine days to the controversy with the A-B-C-D ships.

Ted and I took a few breaks together. Once we went to a Boston Celtics basketball game. The Celtic's Bob Cousy stole the ball, started a fast break for a lay-up but stepped out of bounds. As soon as the referee blew his whistle, the Boston fans booed and threw paper cups on the court. "Leonard, just think," Ted whispered to me, "their stupid votes cancel out our intelligent votes. Do you think that's how Kennedy won the election?"

Another event was a speech by James Hoffa, President of the International Brotherhood of Teamsters, entitled "Area Contracts and the Teamsters." It was sponsored by the Harvard Law School and the Harvard Economics Department. Hoffa bragged about how the Teamsters were saving the common truck drivers and our nation from exploitation by greedy capitalists. A member of the audience asked why the Teamsters picketed his father's small moving company and bankrupted the family business. Hoffa replied, "I don't negotiate contracts. Ask the starving truck drivers on the picket lines." The audience broke out in cheers and clapped for Hoffa. I thought of our company's recent problem with the Teamsters. "Ted, now you know," I growled. "These left-leaning, trust-fund liberals in cahoots with the blind Boston Celtics fans put Kennedy into office." I didn't mention Mother's Catholic vote.

Meanwhile, my family and business responsibilities continued but with a major difference—my parents began to pressure me to hurry up and finish my dissertation. After a telephone call from Dad in late March 1962, I wrote him: "I sometimes feel . . . that there is a growing disappointment with my contributions to the company and with the time it is taking me to earn my degree. Believe me when I say that I am working as rapidly and as earnestly as possible. But historical research by the very nature of the material being hard to uncover is slow; if the material and facts were out in the open for anyone to stumble on, someone earlier would have written the book. All in all, I am progressing toward the degree and I am not about to do a slipshod job or to take a chance of having my thesis rejected because I rushed through. There is too much time and sweat invested for me to give up or lower my standard of work now. In the meantime I can squeeze in any special work that you have for me; I am more than willing to do whatever you ask and whatever I am capable of doing. Naturally that decision is yours and yours alone to make."

Later Mother revealed their feelings in general. "Dad's very downhearted," she wrote; "I've never seen him so down cast since his Mother died. That goes for me too. It seems the more we work, the further down we are pushed by all concerned and it's to the point where Dad and I have to start to think of ourselves, health wise as well as money wise."

Dad and Mother seemed to be going through a stereotypical mid-life crisis. Dad became obsessed with his childhood dream of flying. He took flying lessons, received his pilot's license, bought his own single-engine plane, began flying solo and disappeared often for the entire day. With a restricted license, he had to fly solo because he was not experienced enough to carry passengers. So Mother stayed home and sulked.

Mother's obsession shifted from Beat poets to acquiring a beach house at the New Jersey shore. My parents purchased in late 1961 a cottage at Forked River, New Jersey, which Mother spent the next six months repainting and refurnishing. Dad was flying and Mother was redecorating. Not only were they isolating themselves from each other, but also they were neglecting the day-to-day activities at the company.

Grandma Brey, age 75 and now living with my parents, was discovered babbling and wandering down Route 663. Everyone feared the onset of dementia or Alzheimer's. It turned out that Grandma Brey, who was adamantly opposed to drinking alcohol, had been secretly buying Robitussin, which had an alcohol content of seven percent, and drinking it by the bottle. In the storage area next to her bedroom were cardboard cartons in which she had hidden hundreds of empty bottles. When Mother cut off her Robitussin, Grandma started screaming "Don't be fussin' with my tussin' or you'll hear my cussin'!" and refused to come out of her room. "Schnitzel happens!" Mother responded.

Judy and the girls were living their lives. They spent the entire summer of 1962 vacationing at the Forked River cottage and enjoying the sun and sand. I saw them on the occasional weekend. When we returned to Cambridge, Debby and now Rachael attended the Leslie-Ellis School. Judy finally had her days free and did her thing—obsessively sewing dress after dress for the girls, playing folk ballads on her guitar and shopping for bargains at Filene's basement.

In September 1962, Ted Sloan and I went to Washington, D.C. to research in the National Archives on Benjamin Franklin Isherwood and John Roach. While bunking at the Washington YMCA, I received an unexpected letter from Judy. "I miss you Leonard," she gushed, "and I love you very much, even though you are grouchy . . . see you soon, sweet dreams, love, Judy." It was strange. It was only the second letter that I had received from her ever; and the first one had been the circle letter from high school.

Returning to Cambridge for Registration on September 21, I eventually heard what was happening. The retching noise in the morning from the bathroom confirmed that Judy was pregnant. Given my schedule, I was suspicious that I was not the father. But who? Guitar teacher? Hippie poet? Bridge partner? Pizza boy at Forked River? The author of my indignation didn't merit investigation. I flipped my mental switch to "off" and the marriage was over. The details could be worked out after I graduated. I would join the ranks of the lepers with my Uncle Preston. I would continue my record of the youngest Swann married and the youngest Swann father and would add to it, the youngest Swann divorced.

My Mother visited Cambridge and discovered my "problem." She had to consult with Dad. "We have been giving your problem a lot of thought," wrote Mother, "and I'm saying a novena to St. Jude for you. Dad and I . . . wish things were different, but if this is the way it will have to be, so be it. We will stick with you all the way." St. Jude didn't intervene to change my mind. The switch remained "off."

Now my concentration was on completing my thesis on John Roach and defending it before the Academic Committee, securing my Ph.D. and escaping the mutual hostilities at Fernald Drive. Theresa Swavely, a long-time office employee at the oil company, volunteered to type the draft and redraft.

Coincidentally, I had met our new neighbor across the street, Dolores Ackel Fiore, at Leslie-Ellis School. Her son Paul Ernest was also enrolled there, and our children occasionally commuted together. Dolores had a Ph.D. in Romance Languages from the joint Harvard-Radcliffe program; was teaching Spanish at Boston College, a Jesuit institution; and was researching Reuben Dario, a Nicaraguan poet who initiated the Spanish American modernismo literary movement. In return for my taking Paul with Debby and Rachael to school in the morning, Dolores offered to proof read my thesis and make editorial suggestions. I began visiting her apartment, and together we edited my drafts spread over her kitchen table. After my Mother, she was the smartest woman whom I had ever met. I learned that she was separated from her husband. Gradually, our relationship developed but we delayed serious talk about a future until both our divorces were final.

"John Roach, Maritime Entrepreneur," my thesis, 420 pages, was delivered to the Department of History on the first Monday of April, 1963. The next step was a Final Examination, really an oral defense of my thesis before a Committee of two independent experts from outside the Harvard Community. I waited and waited for the scheduling of that Final Examination. Nothing happened. I began to panic. On May 20, a letter arrived from Robert Wolff, Chairman of the Department of History, which stated: "I am happy to inform you that you will not be required to take a 'special' examination for the Ph. D. degree. Since your thesis has been approved, this means that all requirements have been completed." Later, Professor Albion told me that my thesis had been accepted and complimented by the independent experts, who had found it professional, thorough and convincing and therefore had waived the oral defense. Subsequently, The United States Naval Institute published my thesis as a book without changing one word.

My academic life at Harvard was finished. My parents attended the Graduation ceremonies on June 13, 1963—ironically David's birthday—and witnessed my receiving a Doctor of Philosophy degree in History. As I clutched my certificate and listened to the assembly sing "Fair Harvard," I was saddened by the opening line of the second stanza—"Farewell! be thy destinies onward and bright!"

But my destiny was anything but bright. Judy had delivered a son, Paul Alexander, on May 3, 1963, in a Boston hospital and had refused to admit me into the delivery room or her hospital room. As soon as she was ready to be released, she had been rescued by her Father, had grabbed Debby and Rachael—and the Mercedes—and had departed for the garage apartment in Zionsville. I never saw the baby boy. Dad's mantra was ringing in my ear—"Never let the bastards"—or in this case the female equivalent—"get you down and never, never let the S.O.B's know that you are hurting."

Return Days

There I was, part Tin Man and part Cowardly Lion, sitting alone, in summer 1963, staring at a blank wall in a sterile two-room apartment, located over a real estate office in Pottstown. My Mother had found the apartment for me and furnished it with a second-hand bed, dresser, kitchen table and two kitchen chairs. The only decoration was a small statue of St. Francis of Assisi, which Mother had given me as a house-warming present since St. Jude had not been effective in my recent past.

My Dad and Mother were hopping around in their Cessna or trolling from their fishing boat off the coast of New Jersey or eating seafood at their cottage at Forked River. David was backpacking with college friends across Europe. Judy was firing up her lawyer and denying me visits with my daughters. Dolores was researching for her book on Ruben Dario in South America. My only commitment outside the usual oil business was to start in the fall semester as a Lecturer on American History at Drexel Institute of Art, Science and Industry in Philadelphia. Professor Freidel had arranged this position for me with his friend, the Chairman of the History Department there.

So I pulled a Jack Kerouac. I got a passport and headed for São Paulo, Brazil, to catch up with Dolores and her son Paul. We traveled to Rio de Janeiro, where the high-rise buildings stood in contrast to the favelas. We ate feijoados on Ipanimo Beach, where I was surprised by the nude sunbathers. We flew to Buenos Aires and mingled with the gauchos; then on to Lima and the Inca ruins at Machu Piachu. It was my first adult impulsive act, my first foreign trip, my first real vacation and my first leap into a new commitment. Dolores and I agreed to marry as soon as legally possible.

Then I returned for my first employment outside the family business. In a metropolitan area with the University of Pennsylvania, LaSalle University, Temple University, Saint Joseph's University,

Villanova University, Immaculata University, West Chester University, Philadelphia College of Art, Haverford College, Bryn Mahr College, Swathmore College and Widener College, Drexel Institute was known as the school for engineers and medical technicians. Drexel's unique cooperative program had its students alternate semesters, studying one semester on campus and then working the next semester as a full-time trainee in companies that embraced their technical career interests. Thus, Drexel students usually enrolled in the introductory American History course only to fulfill a requirement for a credit in humanities for graduation.

Mirroring the enthusiasm of my Muhlenberg and Harvard professors but minimizing date-laden lectures, I shared the stories as experienced and reported by the actual participants in the ebb and flow of historical events. "Give me liberty or give me death," shouted Patrick Henry to lead the American Revolution. Honest Abraham Lincoln called for the abolition of slavery: "A house divided against itself cannot stand." Mary Ellen Lease, the "Kansas Pythoness," agitated her fellow farmers in the Populist Movement with her rant "To raise less corn and more hell." Jerry Simpson, the Populist candidate from Kansas for Congress, mocked his opponent's silk stockings as proof of aristocracy. "Sockless Jerry," the Socrates of the Prairie, was elected. In their exams, every student quoted Patrick Henry, Honest Abe, the Kansas Pythoness and Sockless Jerry.

My life on the faculty was rarely idealistic but overwhelmingly mundane. One entire department meeting consisted of a heated argument over who should receive the $100 grant to attend a conference at Colonial Williamsburg; the idealistic academics fought over a Benjamin. Virtually no opportunity existed for a lowly lecturer to fast track to a tenured position. My salary was miserly and barely covered my support obligations, apartment rent and gasoline money, let alone the occasional low-fare commuter flight between Newark, New Jersey, and Boston for a weekend with Dolores. And in addition, the problems in the family oil company were demanding more attention and energy. "It is rather difficult," the psychiatrist had written in my "Vocational Guidance Report," to Harvard, "to combine academic teaching with business pursuits . . . one or the other of these activities could become the preferred one . . . the incompatibility will resolve itself." And it did. I decided after one year to abandon teaching at Drexel and join the family business full time.

Swann Oil, Inc. in 1964 was remarkably different from the dump truck that Dad drove after World War II. When Dad returned from the Navy, his first regular job was as a girder painter for Bethlehem Steel in Pottstown, and his Sunday job was working as engineer for the sound system at Hickory Park for its cowboy music shows. In 1948, Uncle Joe gave him a dump truck, which Dad drove to develop a one-man business delivering coal to the farmers and residents around Sassamansville, hauling quarry stones for building retaining walls and houses, top soil for lawns, yellow gravel for driveways, neighbor's trash to the landfill and for plowing snow from country roads. It required a hustle to keep that dump truck moving.

Gasoline for the dump truck came from Uncle Joe's tank at his Sassamansville maintenance garage. In late 1948, the delivery man for the Atlantic Refining Company, Uncle Joe's supplier, mentioned to Dad that Atlantic planned to stop delivering to its country customers and was looking to establish a local distributer. Dad hurried to the Atlantic corporate office in Philadelphia and secured the distributorship with its few existing customers. Uncle Joe supplied a loan to convert the dump truck by removing the dump body from the chassis and replacing it with an old tanker body from an abandoned Atlantic Refining Company's truck, a four compartment 1000-gallon-capacity tank. Dad cashed in his G.I. insurance policy for $200 as his working capital. Dad was now in business as L.A. Swann Atlantic Products, a sole proprietorship with one old truck and one employee—Dad—who would drive to the Atlantic pipeline terminal at Exton, about 30 miles south of Sassamansville, for his supply of kerosene, fuel oil, and gasoline. A staple of his business was to supply kerosene to the farmers. There was no meter on the old tank. So Dad filled a five gallon bucket, dumped it into the farmer's storage tank (usually a 55 gallon drum) and turned a dial one notch on the tanker door for each bucket poured to calculate the bill.

Starting with the few accounts turned over by Atlantic, Dad expanded to fuel oil and more gasoline; and the business grew one account at a time—Erb's Country Store, Bauman's Apple Butter Plant, the Lodge where the Boy Scout troop met, and the Pennsylvania Dutch farmers—the Renningers, Kulps, Slonakers and Yoders. Soon added to the growing customer base were Hickory Park Restaurant; St. Phillip

Neri Church and the Green Lane Church; the diner where the Knights of Columbus, a Catholic prayer fraternity, held their breakfast meetings; and even the pocketbook factory in Pennsburg where Grandma Brey now labored as a sewing machine operator.

The key was dependable service. Father Letterhouse, other acquaintances of the family, and the local farmers could look the country boy in the eye and know that they could count on him. Moreover, after the war there was a rush to convert the old, dusty coal furnaces to burn fuel oil. Everyone was reading the newspaper stories about the new housing developments, such as Levittown, where hundreds and hundreds of cookie-cutter houses were built with the new heating systems powered by fuel oil. The fuel oil business grew. One truck with a pump and a meter was added. A Renninger came aboard as the first employee and then a Schoenly was added as the second delivery man. Mother was overwhelmed with the bookkeeping but still implemented a primitive degree-day system to predict oil consumption to schedule deliveries so that the customer would not run out of fuel oil.

One logistical problem was running the small tank trucks on 60-mile round trips to Atlantic's Exton pipeline terminal to pick up the product. Not only was it time consuming and costly, but also driving over the winding, hilly two-lane road in snowy and icy weather was unpredictable and dangerous. Dad purchased two acres down the street from our bungalow and erected a small storage terminal consisting of one 20,000-gallon above-ground tank and four 10,000-gallon above-ground tanks for fuel oil, kerosene and two grades of gasoline. In front of the storage terminal, he had Weller and Updegrove, contractor friends from Gilbertsville, built a cement-block garage with three truck-bays and an attached office; and to the side they constructed a brick two-story house for our family.

To supply the storage terminal an International tractor and a 6,000-gallon tank trailer were added to the growing truck fleet. Irvin Lloyd became the company's first tractor-trailer driver. Soon a Mack tractor and trailer were purchased, and Liver was the driver. Liver never used a last name.

Domestic oil burners required service—normal maintenance to keep them running efficiently and emergency service when they broke down. Bill Berkey was hired as the first oil burner mechanic and a panel truck purchased from Quigley Motors in Bally was his service vehicle.

Then Carl Hartman came on board as the second oil-burner serviceman. Service contacts opened opportunities to sell steel oil storage tanks. "Oh, you have this small 55-gallon drum for your kerosene, why not buy a 275-gallon tank? . . . Your 275-gallon fuel oil tank needs a paint job, why not consider buying a 550 or 1000-gallon underground tank. You coat it once with tar-based paint and then bury the tank in the ground . . . plus you get a discount for the quantity purchase of fuel oil and you can fill up in the summer when fuel oil prices are lower . . . you have peace of mind because you have adequate supply in the snowy winter months." I learned that spiel to sell many, many fuel oil tanks and to secure larger orders for fuel oil delivery.

The vacant garage bays in the daytime bothered Dad, the same way a tongue constantly sliding across a chipped molar is annoying. So Dad decided to sell car tires, truck tires and tractor tires and use that space for changing tires in the daytime. He secured distributorships from Lee Tire Company and Firestone Tire and Rubber Company. With ready access to the Firestone manufacturing plant in Pottstown, he didn't have to maintain a big inventory but could still give quick service on replacement tires. Firestone's development of the Town and Country snow tire added another boost to his tire sales.

With home heating oil sales growing, Dad in the mid-1950's purchased three acres across the street and had Fisher Tank Company erect a million-gallon ground storage tank. His economic strategy was country smart. Retail fuel oil business was slow in the summer months when demand was down. The refineries traditionally lowered wholesale fuel oil prices by a penny and sometimes more per gallon in the summer months, and for large purchases would defer payment at no interest until October 10. The truck fleet was slow in the summer. So the million-gallon storage tank could be filled in the summer months with fuel oil at a lower wholesale cost, hauled by tractor-trailers that would normally sit idle, driven by truck drivers in good weather with no snow and ice for accidents, plus the drivers were on regular time, not the horrendous overtime of the winter season. Dad's plan was brilliant. For example, if the differential between the summer to winter price were only a penny, the accrued income on the million-gallons was $10,000 minus about $1500 interest for the fall months, plus savings of approximately $4000 in overtime drivers winter wages for a net gain of $12,500. Not to mention, the additional sales pitch to the homeowner—"Look, come kick our tank . . . a million gallons of fuel oil . . . You heard right—a million gallons right here . . . You never have to worry about your fuel oil in the winter time."

"Tomorrow is the big money day," Mother crowed in an October letter, "Dad is going to Philadelphia to pay off the million gallons of oil . . . $100,000 will be paid directly to Pruitt and Atlantic . . . Francis [our billing clerk] is doing a good job, so Dad raised her 10 cents an hour."

Then in mid-1956, with the help of Judy's father, the business expanded into additional products. The Sandura Company's Fullerton plant used No. 6 fuel oil in its manufacturing of sheet vinyl. (In the refining process, crude oil is broken down into a multitude of products including gasoline, light fuel oil, and residual heavy oil products —No.4, No. 5 and No.6 fuel oils. These lower-priced heavier products were used to heat large buildings and for generating energy, both for heating and manufacturing processes in industrial plants.) Sandura's requirements were seven to eight trailer loads (5000 gallons each) of No. 6 fuel oil each week. This was a new business —selling to industrial customers—which required a separate source of supply and additional trailers dedicated to transport only heavy oil. Dad secured an additional Distributorship Agreement with the Atlantic Refining Company for heavy oil and purchased an additional tractor and two trailers dedicated to these products, which were loaded at the Atlantic Refinery in Philadelphia and delivered directly to the customer.

Our industrial and commercial business began a rapid growth. Judy's father convinced the Modern Transport Company to buy its two trailer loads of diesel fuel per week from us. Next, Uncle Jack contacted a retired State Police friend, who was head of security at Western Electric Company in Allentown. Uncle Jack's friend introduced us to the Purchasing Agent at Western Electric, who awarded half of their business, three trailer loads a week to our company. Another retired State Police buddy of Uncle Jack's worked at Keystone Lamp and steered their business of several truck loads a month to us. Uncle Jack had another acquaintance, Rudy Sandowitz, the owner of Quakertown Brick and Tile Company. A few years earlier, Uncle Jack on State Police patrol had pulled over Sandowitz's teenage son for erratic driving. He was under the influence of alcohol. But instead of arresting him, Uncle Jack drove him home in his patrol car. So Sandowitz owed

Uncle Jack a big favor; and our Oil Company shipped four trailer loads each week to fire the kilns at Quakertown Brick. Sandowitz was also on the board of the Jewish Community Center in Allentown; another contract for eight trailer loads a year headed our way. Sandowitz's cousin Morris helped us land the business at the Allentown Hospital. Morris personally recommended our company to the President of the Hospital Board, because, as Rudy explained, "Morris knoss him batter den yous." Another commitment for 50 trailer loads a year resulted from "knoss him batter."

The sales continued. The squeeze-box player at the family jam sessions was a truck driver for Dana Corporation. Its Pottstown plant manufactured automobile parts for the Big Three automobile companies. He introduced Dad to the Purchasing Agent, who also was a polka fanatic and rolled out a contract for 50 trailer loads a year and we had a barrel of business.

Uncle Joe and Dad were members of the Rotary Club in East Greenville. While Uncle Joe as past President and Dad as the current President were at a Rotary Club regional function in Pottstown, they met Tom Storm, the Purchasing Agent for Firestone Tire and Rubber Company. They chatted about the business of selling tires and fuel oil. Tom liked his scotch and hinted that for a case of Chivas Regal at Christmas, Dad could buy all the Town and Country tires he needed directly from the plant (a verbal guarantee of an unlimited supply of a tire in high demand in winter months) and for two cases of Chivas Regal, the entire heavy oil contract of one truck load a day would be awarded to us. Guess who received three cases of Chivas Regal every Christmas until he retired two decades later?

Among Dad's early domestic heating oil customers was the bushy-browed and balding Harry Bertoia. A struggling sculptor, Bertoia had confided to Dad that he was embarrassed because he had no regular income to pay the fuel oil bills for his farm house in Barto and his two-story barn-like studio in Bally. Dad worked out a trade and for years exchanged fuel oil for Bertoia's metal sculptures—musical sculptures and "Small Bush" sculptures made of welded bronze rods. Dad with his musical ear was fascinated by the lyrical notes from the vibrating sculptures. Bertoia also was a designer for Knoll Associates, the manufacturer of avant-garde office furniture. When Bertoia learned that Dad also supplied industrial fuel oil, he encouraged the Knoll manufacturing plant in East Greenville to purchase its requirement from our company and also to give us free samples of their latest Bertoia-designed office desks and chairs.

One day, Dad was at the Pottstown Diner and overheard two fellows in the next booth moaning about problems with the kilns at the Robinson Clay plant, which manufactured culbert-size clay pipes. One was the Plant Manager, who coincidentally Dad remembered from Boyertown High School. Dad interrupted them and said that possibly our service mechanic could help with the problem. Bill Berkey went. He saw. He conquered. We received the Robinson Clay oil business, about 15 truckloads a week.

Uncle Joe's high school buddy was the manager of the Boyertown Burial Casket Company and gave us their fuel oil business. A relative of one of our truck drivers was a Longacre of Longacre's Dairy in Bally; we were awarded their account. A member of Mother's book club had a brother in management at Bally Case and Cooler Company. He heard from his sister about our industrial burner service; we garnered both their service and fuel contracts. Quigley Motors in Bally, where Dad bought our pickup trucks, and Sparr Buick and Pontiac, where Uncle Joe and Dad purchased their family cars, became our customers. And so the stream of industrial and commercial business grew larger.

As the company grew so did the need for more space. Desks for Dad, Mother and two bookkeepers took over the band room in the basement of their house. Ringing telephones and chattering adding machines replaced the guitar riffs of the family jam sessions. But by the early-1960s more physical facilities were needed. Another large building was erected across the street in front of the million-gallon storage tank. This 9,000-square-foot building with brick front and cement block sides, built by Weller and Updegrove, had office space in the front section, drivers lounge and parts storage area next, and then five repair bays large enough for pulling in the entire tractor-trailer. The five above-ground storage tanks were relocated across the street and positioned to the left of the million-gallon tank. Dad also purchased the land between his old white bungalow and this new facility, about four acres, for additional space to park the trucks and for future expansion.

Building the new office seemed to rekindle and revitalize the hustle factor that Dad previously had when operating his dump truck. Dad's hustle was evident in his surprise decision to form a country western band with company employees—Janet Smith, a secretary on vocals à la Patsy Cline (I can still hear her strong voice belting out the classic Patsy Cline song, "Crazy."); Bill Berkey, burner serviceman on base guitar; Bob Marriott, tractor-trailer driver on vocals, guitar and mandolin; Mike Sanders, Sales Manager occasionally on guitar; Sam Shellaway, tractor-trailer driver on accordion; and Dad, lead vocals and lead guitar. The Swann Western Band performed paying gigs on the weekends at local fire houses, wedding receptions and church carnivals.

Dad's hustle was evident in his securing in 1964 a contract, which would utilize a few of the company's tractors at night, with the Post Office Department to pull Post Office trailers full of mail on round-trips between the regional gathering centers in Pottstown and Reading and the main Post Office Distribution Center in Philadelphia.

Dad's hustle was evident in his following up on another contact from Uncle Jack and purchasing the Benninghoff Coal Company in Allentown, a local distributor of coal to domestic customers. The plan was not only to continue running the Benninghoff dump trucks to deliver coal to existing customers, but also eventually to convert those coal customers to fuel oil, plus tap into the existing home heating oil users in the Lehigh Valley. For the acquired Benninghoff property on 14th and Green Streets in Allentown, blueprints were drawn to erect a new office building and a 250,000-gallon ground storage tank for fuel oil. The Allentown City Council revoked the first building permit for the above ground tank when it later decided to build a new Junior High School nearby but then approved a compromise plan for the installation of eight 30,000-gallon underground tanks. Construction of the new Allentown tank facility and a 4,700-square-foot, two-story office building was underway by late 1964.

It was truly amazing. There was no family legacy like the Rockefellers or Duponts to hand down mega business. There was no Skull and Bones Society preparing secretly to take over the world and steer business our way. There was only a bunch of Sassamansville country boys, imaginative, energetic and loyal, who cobbled together a dynamic enterprise, which in the mid-1960s had an annual volume of 12 million gallons of petroleum products and 3000 tons of coal, operated 25 trucks, had 35 employees working from locations in Sassamansville and Allentown and even had its own country western band.

From my grade school years through college life, I was involved one way or another in the family business. While in grade school, I often turned the arrow on the counter as Dad dumped the 5-gallon kerosene buckets. While in High School, I answered the phone, made bank deposits, pumped gas and mounted tires. Then I graduated to cleaning oil burners, driving a fuel oil truck for emergency deliveries, selling fuel oil to home owners, landing the first large industrial accounts though marriage, managing the renewal of industrial contracts, hiring and managing the first outside salesman, writing business plans and most important of all—being Mother and Dad's sounding board about virtually every business development during my Muhlenberg, Harvard and Drexel years.

With my commitment to full-time work at Swann Oil, Dad appointed me Vice President with the responsibility for marketing and developing plans for future growth. My office at Sassamansville had only Knoll furniture. Mother continued to supervise the office staff and to function as the defacto Comptroller. When David finished his Master's Degree at Lehigh University, he set up our first computer/electronics system, the NCR magnetic strip system, at the Sassamansville office. Then, the accounting people relocated to the second floor of the new Allentown office in 1968, where David installed the new IBM-360 system with its punch cards, tape drives and disc drives for the centralized billing and accounting for the entire company. David also managed the Allentown retail business. Dad continued his overall supervision of operations with daily oversight of the dispatching of delivery trucks, burner service and maintenance of the truck fleet.

Mike Sanders and I continued to grow the volume with additional business from Schoeneck Farms in Emmaus, Randolph Metals in Phoenixville, Doehler Jarvis in Stowe, the Metropolitan Edison power plants in Reading, Bernadine Sisters Convent in Reading and Mack Trucks in Allentown (we now bought only Mack tractors). As Mike Sanders often said, "With the data I'm collecting, the contacts being made and your sales ability—I'm hoping that Swann Oil will grow considerably."

Cygnet Chemical Company—a subtle baby swan reference—was formed to market to our industrial customers a chemical additive to increase the clean-burning characteristic of heavy oil. The patent for this proprietary product was purchased from a local inventor.

Cygnet's office was across the street in the old dispatcher's office; and the manager was Alma Coggins, a talented artist who created floral oil paintings. Jack Coggins, her husband, was an artist historian. He had been an artist correspondent in the United States Army and drew battle illustrations from his duty on the front lines in World War II. His illustrated history books were <u>Arms and Equipment of the Civil War</u>, published in 1962; <u>The Fighting Man</u>, 1966; and <u>Ships and Seaman of the American Revolution</u>, 1969. The Coggins lived on a farm in Berks County, about five miles west of Sassamansville, and became my good friends.

In the midst of all this business activity, I had to sort out my personal life. Judy's lawyer was pushing for both alimony and support for three children. I asked Uncle Jack if he could help secure evidence of her infidelity. His angry advice was to ignore my suspicions and disregard her lawyer—"You can always tell when a lawyer is lying—It's when his lips are moving!"—and to work out a settlement. The final agreement included alimony to end if Judy remarried; support for all three children and her ownership of the Mercedes. Our divorce became final in late 1963.

Judy, over the years, became a serial monogamist, who as the post-Cambridge, sophisticated "Judith" changed her marital name from Swann to Schaible to Barrow to Hughes to Curtis to Doan. Judith's peregrinations, my focus on establishing another family and my frenetic business activities would restrict my contact with Debby and Rachael. However, in addition to child support, I voluntarily paid for Debby and Rachael's education at private schools and colleges.

I had returned from my adventure in South America thoroughly committed to Dolores. In that relaxed atmosphere she had spontaneously dropped a few background details. Her grandfather, a Maronite Catholic, had emigrated from Zahle', Lebanon, to Brockton, Massachusetts. Her father had died at an early age, leaving her mother and older brother to raise her and two younger siblings. Proficient in Latin, Spanish and Portuguese, Dolores had secured her Ph. D. in Romance Languages through the joint Harvard-Radcliffe program. Pregnant with Paul, she had married her Italian boyfriend from Brooklyn, who had just received a Harvard Law Degree and an entry position at a New York Law firm. They had separated when he decided to abandon the practice of law and return to manage the family's shoe manufacturing plant. Dolores had moved back to Cambridge when she secured the position to teach Introductory Spanish at Boston College.

We mused about becoming the next famous husband and wife writing team, perhaps the next Oscar and Mary Handlin or the next Robert Albion and Jennie Barnes Pope. However, her obsession with Rubin Dario did not mesh with my concentration in Maritime History. We talked about both of us teaching at the College level. We talked about her moving to Philadelphia where she felt confident in finding a position with all the universities and colleges in the area. However, she would only move if I agreed to provide her dream house in the Main Line area of Philadelphia.

With Uncle Joe's real estate acumen, a perfect one-and-a-half acre lot was found at 1100 Brynllawn Road in Villanova. It was purchased in January 1964 by Swann Realty, Inc. Weller and Updegrove began construction of a 3500-square-foot brick colonial house (two stories and finished basement, nine rooms, four bathrooms, maid's quarters and two-car garage).

In July 1964, we were married in Elkton, Maryland, where a Justice of the Peace could marry you immediately if you presented a birth certificate and proof of divorce. It was a total surprise to learn from her birth certificate that Dolores was seven years older than I!

Dolores and Paul moved to Brynllawn Road in the summer of 1965; and our dream existence in our dream house began. Our daughter, Heather Marina, was born on February 22, 1966. I was so excited that I drove past the exit for the Philadelphia Hospital, wound up on the bridge leading to New Jersey, and heard 15 versions of "Stupid Bastard" in four languages as we barely found the hospital in time. I suggested the name, Heather Marina, because I wanted the familiar nautical ring—"HMS." Our son, Leonard Alexander III—Tres—was born on January 5, 1970. (Again, I got lost on the way to the hospital.) I insisted on the name, Leonard Alexander, for obvious lineage reasons. I was very content with my life that now combined exciting business activities in the day and dreams at home at night.

"I have spread my dreams under your feet," W. B. Yeats wrote. "Tread softly because you tread on my dreams." There was the occasional reality tread on my dreams. When Dolores moved to Villanova, she transformed herself into a Boston Brahman complete with an exaggerated "Haarvad" and "paak tha caar" accent and compulsively needed to exhibit her egotistical superiority over the Philadelphia Main Line Matrons. At first, it was amusing. Here was this poor Lebanese-American from Brockton, which was the equivalent of being Pennsylvania Dutch from Bally, itching to challenge the proud descendants of William Penn.

Dolores announced that she "didn't do housework" and she "didn't do babies." So we had to have a live-in au pair—always a foreigner on a temporary visa—for the daytime. I took care of the feeding, changing diapers and lullabies for Heather and Tres at night.

But she did supervise the preparation and sometimes cooked the evening meal. For the next 16 years when she actually cooked, it was usually the same menu of sirloin steak, baked potato and peas, which we had to eat at the formal dining room table, with my wearing a coat and tie; and everyone had to report and discuss the inane events of his day.

Disturbing was her obsession with dogs—first dachshunds and later German Shepherds. In Sassamansville, dogs were for hunting and guarding outside, not invited guests with complete run of the house. Dolores' tolerance for slobbering tongues, fugitive hairs and unpredictable gross schedules was in marked contrast to her intolerance for a mispronounced Latin word, wrinkled bed sheet or unopened car door.

More disturbing was her micromanagement of Paul's education; it was so intensive that it made a helicopter parent seem benign. Paul was enrolled in Episcopal Academy, ranked among the best on the Main Line. Every night, Dolores reviewed his homework and was particularly critical of his Latin. If Paul made a mistake in declining or conjugating a Latin word, she literally became Brutus, screaming and punching him. Then, the next day after school, she would take Paul to Kiddie City to pick out a game or puzzle. Scores and scores of games and puzzles were stacked in the closets in Paul's bedroom.

Perhaps most surprising was her abandonment of her academic teaching or writing interests. She didn't submit one application for a teaching position at any of the 13 local universities or colleges. When I heard that Immaculata University was interviewing for a Spanish Professor, she refused to send in her application. Nor did she continue her research on Rubin Dario. In fact, I never saw research files or notebooks on Rubin Dario. This was particularly inexplicable since I still had contact with the academic world. I talked often to Professors Victor Johnson, Robert Albion and Frank Freidel, had a research grant from the Naval Historical Foundation for a history of the Brooklyn Navy Yard and continued part-time research for that book. Also, I maintained casual contact with the local education community. For instance, I gave the Welcoming Speech on the merits of a Liberal Arts Education to Muhlenberg Freshmen in 1969. "Your experience here," I pontificated, "will expand your imagination, stimulate your curiosity, create a historical awareness, provide touchstones to evaluate options, and hopefully breed a sense of humility."

By that Liberal Arts definition—except the humility part—our marriage overall was good. I had a partner for intellectual conversation in the evening; and, as Uncle Joe would say, a partner for "schmoozing" in multiple tongues with the officials from the foreign refineries producing the surplus of heavy fuel oil that our company needed. The "schmoozing" decade was about to begin.

Entrepreneurial Days

There I was in early 1970, part Captain Ahab and part Captain Kirk, at age 31 the newly appointed president of Swann Oil, Inc., on a plane to the Midwest to discuss a real estate deal with a Fortune 500 Company. Uncle Joe, the family real estate expert, had located an ideal waterfront property—44 acres at 67th Street and the Schuylkill River in the heart of the Philadelphia Refinery District. The property was zoned to permit the construction of a refinery and petroleum terminal. The Schuylkill River had a 35-feet-deep channel, deep enough for an ocean-going tanker lifting 200,000 barrels (at 42 gallons per barrel, 8,400,000 gallons) of heavy fuel oil. About one block to the south of the property were three pipelines—the main trunk of the Atlantic Keystone Pipeline; the Colonial Pipeline for connections to the Gulf Coast refineries; and the Buckeye pipeline—important logistical connections to move No.2 fuel oil and gasoline, both into the prospective terminal and out to inland terminals. There was also a railroad siding. The property was perfect for the next step in our company's growth.

Over the whish of the jet engines, I marveled how postured, positioned, and prepared I was for this tactical step. I thought about John Roach's vertical integration but in reverse—now integrating backwards from customer to transportation to supply. I labeled it "Reverse Integration." I thought about Professor Robert Albion's core premise in "Boats" that added value comes from moving the supply of material from the source to the market demand by marine transportation at the lowest cost.

My strategic analysis started with the growing demand for low-sulphur, heavy fuel oils from the industrial plants in the Eastern United States; this demand came from expansion in the economy and from the conversion from coal to fuel oil as the primary power source. The domestic refineries basically ignored this growing industrial demand because the greatest profit from refining a barrel of crude oil resulted from higher yields of gasoline, diesel fuel and home heating oil. Technological advances concentrated on increasing the yield of the lighter products. Moreover, the small yield of heavy oils being produced by the major domestic refineries in the Gulf Coast was distant from the growing industrial market on the East Coast and had to be transported by law on United States flag vessels, crewed by United States maritime unions, at high freight costs.

Foreign refineries were still producing a good supply of heavy oils but had limited domestic markets. Supply of heavy oils in Europe and South America outweighed demand. The major United States oil companies often ignored the foreign supply because under United States Import Quotas it was more profitable to import crude oil for higher refining profits than heavy fuel oil. The opportunity existed—so obvious to any student in "Boats"—for an independent marketer to move the foreign surplus supply by foreign-flag ocean tankers with the lowest transportation costs to the United States market.

While the strategy was simple, the tactical implementation required multiple components coming together: a foreign refining supply of heavy fuel oil; deep-water terminal with heated storage tanks for heavy fuel oil; access to foreign-flag ocean tankers; specialized barges with heating coils for intercostal movement of heavy fuel oil; a tractor-trailer delivery fleet; specialized industrial burner service; and, of course, a base of industrial customers. Our family business had a growing industrial customer base. Now the plan was to integrate backwards. Starting that integration was the purpose of my trip.

The property was perfect for the first major step in our plan. Uncle Joe had tracked down the Real Estate Manager who encouraged us with "Yes, the property might be for sale if the price were right." His definition of "Right" was $2 million and our definition, $1 million. In my negotiating visit to his office, I noticed that the walls reeked of hunting trophies—deer and moose antlers, bear paws, stuffed ducks and geese—luckily no swans. As he made small talk about his recent hunt from a duck blind in the marshes of Louisiana, he mentioned that as he quacked to lure the ducks to fly by, he dreamed his weapon was an over-and-under shotgun. I ran with his dream to Uncle Jack, who knew a gun dealer with the rare over-and-under shotgun. A counter offer was made; a shotgun delivered; a contract signed; and a waterfront property acquired. It is still frightening to realize that the company's future turned—not on Harvard intellect—but on an over-and-under shotgun.

Purchasing the property was only the beginning. We needed substantial long-term financing—a long-term mortgage of $5 million to construct the terminal. The Philadelphia Industrial Development Authority and a consortium of three Philadelphia banks turned down our loan application in 24 hours. They reasoned that country boys from Sassamansville could not compete with four major refineries located in the Philadelphia area, which was the second largest refining complex in the United States, as evidenced by the historical fact that no independent company had ever built a deep-water terminal in the Philadelphia harbor.

The American Bank and Trust Company in Reading rescued the project with a long-term mortgage. The American Bank was impressed by our company's customer base in the Reading area. Jack Guerin, Manager of Purchasing at Metropolitan Edison Company, sent a reference letter on how important and indispensable Swann Oil was as its supplier of the critical fuel oils needed for the electric generating plants. Even Sister Edmundine of the Bernadine Convent wrote a letter on the reliability of our industrial burner service and fuel deliveries for the secure tranquility of the convent. The American Bank reasoned that a local supplier of industrial fuel oils would be a major asset for attracting new business to the Reading Area.

Our Schuylkill River terminal was designed primarily by Jack Tyrrell, an engineer who soon would join our company. The initial plans called for 750,000 barrels of fuel oil storage. Fisher Tank Company, the same fabricator of our Sassamansville million-gallon tank, erected the tanks. Weller and Updegrove, Dad's friends who built our Sassamanville office, constructed the office building and attached maintenance garage.

While construction was underway, Ashland Refining Company of Kentucky contacted me. Ashland wanted to expand its sale of gasoline to independent service stations in the Philadelphia area and compete with the entrenched local refineries. Attracted by the logistics of our new terminal, with deep-water and pipeline connections, and our independent, good-old-boy country status, Ashland entered into a long-term lease for two gasoline storage tanks and through-put access to load their trucks. Two additional tanks and gasoline capability were added to our build schedule.

As the welding torches were sizzling, Uncle Jack, now a Captain in the Pennsylvania State Police and scheduled to retire in late 1972, insisted that I meet Joe Flynn, a newcomer to his weekly poker games. As the Purchasing Agent for Wyomising Steel Company, a small steel mill in suburban Philadelphia, Joe awarded us his contract for eight tractor-trailer loads a week of a special grade of low-sulfur No. 6 fuel oil, a unique product required by all steel mills. Perhaps his poker debt to Uncle Jack influenced his quick decision but, lucky for us, it introduced us to a new requirement for this unique product that was in short supply from the domestic refineries. Another tank for low-sulphur No. 6 fuel oil was added to our build schedule so that Swann Oil could import that product. When our Schuylkill River terminal was completed in early 1973, it had 12 storage tanks with over a million barrels of capacity.

Call it Irish luck, but Joe Flynn lost his purchasing position when his steel mill merged with a larger company. I hired Joe as our Sales Specialist for Steel Mills, since he was part of the informal fraternity of steel-mill purchasing agents. Backed by our supply of low-sulphur oil, Joe secured contracts from every steel mill in the tri-state area of Pennsylvania, New Jersey and Delaware; for instance, orders were received for two trailer loads a day from Alan Wood Steel Company in Conshocken and 12 trailer loads a day, seven days a week, from Bethlehem Steel Corporation in Bethlehem.

So much was happening, with parallel, crisscrossing and skyrocketing momentum, that anyone living outside my brain might become confused. I hired John Stathis, in 1972, to open our office at 299 Park Avenue, New York City. John, of Greek heritage, was a specialist in foreign fuel oil supply and ocean transportation. We negotiated a 3-year charter for the *Evgenia K. Chimples*, a Greek-flagged tanker vessel, 555 feet long and drawing 25 feet in draft, that carried 140,000 barrels of fuel oil. It was perfect for the shallow harbor of many foreign refineries and for delivery of foreign fuel oil to our prospective coastal customers and our planned terminals.

I set up Oil Shipping Corporation, an offshore entity for handling our foreign-flag shipping—primarily for administering the spot charters of foreign-flag tankers—and located its corporate office in the IBM Building, Nassau, Bahamas Islands. Henry Hill was hired as manager.

Then I purchased the McKay Insurance Agency to secure a broker's insurance license, thus permitting the direct placement of liability and cargo insurance through our Nassau office to underwriters at Lloyd's of London. Brian Graves of the British firm, Hogg Robinson, became our broker at Lloyd's.

Targeting the market for bunker fuel to foreign-flag vessels in the Philadelphia and New York harbors—now that I had John Stathis' help with the Greek ship owners—I purchased a used tugboat and 20,000-barrel barge with an internal heating system, and based them at our Schuykill River terminal. The tugboat was renamed the *Lottie Swann*, after my grandmother.

A study of oil terminals on the East Coast revealed a lacuna at the port of Savannah, Georgia, and along the Savannah River. There was no heavy oil terminal there to support the growing industries. Swann Oil Company of Georgia, a wholly-owned subsidiary of Swann Oil, purchased an eight-acre tract on the Savannah River at Augusta, Georgia, and constructed a 150,000 barrel terminal and office-maintenance garage, in 1973, at a cost of $2 million. In addition to water access, the terminal was connected to the Colonial Pipeline. Financing was secured through the Development Authority of Richmond County. David moved to Augusta to manage that operation.

The company built a tugboat, the *Marie Swann*, specifically designed to navigate the Savannah River. This 1,000 horsepower, pusher-type, shallow-draft tugboat would move our new specifically-designed barge for use on the snaky Savannah River. With special bow thrusters to navigate the tight curves on the Savannah River, the barge *Swann 18* was 296 feet long, 54 feet wide, had a draft of 7-1/2 feet and a capacity of 16,500 barrels of fuel oil. It had an internal heating system for heavy oil. Also, the flat, open deck of the *Swann 18* was designed to carry 800 tons of deck cargo, trailer boxes and conex boxes, on the return voyage downriver to Savannah. It was the largest barge in history to sail between Savannah and Augusta with one leg of the trip taking three days. This tug-barge unit reopened water transportation on the upper Savannah River, which had seen no commercial traffic in decades.

Next, we purchased land with a deep-water dock used for unloading containers in Savannah and constructed 300,000 barrels of tanks for fuel oils. Ted Bishop, a former Sinclair manager, was hired to supervise that terminal. Swann Oil became the first company in Georgia to combine deep-water port and pipeline deliveries of fuel oil and became the first supplier of industrial fuels located in Georgia. By another stroke of good fortune, a Savannah bank had foreclosed on a 10-acre track of low-cost housing next to our new Savannah terminal and offered it to us for the assumption of the remaining mortgage. It was a great deal that provided both a self-liquidating, income producing property and adjacent land for future expansion of that terminal.

Dad always preached that the key to landing a new customer was "talk less and listen more." To his advice, I added "observe more." Our decision to expand to the Georgia market in 1973 hinged on two key accounts: Continental Can Company with its large plant at Port Wentworth on the Savannah River and Phillip Morris with its tobacco gathering facility near Augusta. On my visit with John Heimlich, the Manager of Energy Purchases, at Continental Can's corporate office in Greenwich, Connecticut, John discussed that his major concern was a secure supply at a competitive price, because without fuel oil they might have to shut down some of their plants in Georgia. I pointed out that our deep-water terminal down river at Savannah would allow us to use our shallow-draft oil tanker, the *Evgenia K. Climples*, which lifted 140,000 barrels at 25 feet draft, to either stop first to unload half of the cargo at our terminal and then continue upstream with the remaining cargo for delivery to Continental Can at its Port Wentworth plant, or to deliver the entire load directly to Continental Can. Thus, Continental Can could receive the lowest delivered price calculated on cargo quantities, plus there was the additional security of fuel oil at our local terminal for emergency barge deliveries, if required. In addition, our firm was building a shallow draft barge and tugboat for use on the Savannah River that would be available if Continental Can required an emergency delivery.

As we talked, I observed that his hands were rough and stained. Was he a mechanic as a hobby? His wife had died recently, he relayed sadly, and to help his teenage sons occupy their evenings and to strengthen their family bond, they were completely rebuilding a Corvette and doing the engine overhaul on their kitchen floor. But he had a problem; he could not find all the used engine parts they needed for the repair. Dad had Russell Ux, our head mechanic at Sassamansville, track down a used Corvette engine in a scrap yard in Phoenixville, which we delivered to Connecticut. So by listening and observing, another pivotal customer was secured. The *Evgenia K. Chimples* delivered our first cargo to Continental Can at Port Wentworth in July 1973.

Phillip Morris had a major tobacco collection facility outside of Augusta and its primary manufacturing plant near Richmond, Virginia. In my meeting in their corporate offices on Park Avenue, I, as a nonsmoker, walked into a possible ambush. The first order of business at the conference table was to pass around a tray with all the Phillip Morris brands so that everyone could light up. I grabbed my unlit cigarette and then waved it, à la my Hugh Heffner pipe movements from High School, to emphasize my answers to their concerns. The construction of our shallow draft tugboats and barges, our terminals at Savannah and Augusta, and our plans for terminals at Chesapeake and Richmond gave the security of localized supply that was necessary for a long-term contract with Phillip Morris. Also, our New York office was up the street at 299 Park Avenue. We were available for face-to-face meetings whenever Phillip Morris needed them. Hugh Heffner and High School dramatics sealed this carton.

Our next move was into Tidewater Virginia, in 1975, by purchasing the old Phillips Petroleum Company's deep-water terminal on the Elizabeth River in Chesapeake, with 92 acres of land, and immediately starting construction of additional heated tankage for the storage of heavy oil and asphalt, which increased the total tank capability to 860,000 barrels. Next we bought the old Atlantic Refining Company's terminal outside Richmond and built additional tanks for heavy oil storage, which increased the total storage capacity to 280,000 barrels. Both terminals were linked to the Colonial Pipeline. Constructed at the same time were the tugboat *Maggie Swann*, named after Grandma Brey, and the *Swann 20*, a 20,000 barrel, heated barge for heavy oil deliveries up river to Richmond and for bunker fuel deliveries to ships in the Hampton Roads harbor. Swann Oil now could supply industrial customers in Virginia and North Carolina, thus adding to our initial customer base of the Phillip Morris plant in Richmond and the Anheuser-Busch brewery in Williamsburg. We also began designing a 26,000 barrel per day refinery for the Chesapeake property.

With our terminals, tug boats and barges in three major harbors—Philadelphia, Hampton Roads and Savannah—Swann Oil was positioned as a dependable supplier of bunker fuel to the foreign flag vessels delivering and loading cargo in those ports. With our office at 299 Park Avenue, we could meet with the ship owners or their New York agents to seal the transactions.

Asphalt and Petroleum Company, Northeast Industrial Oil Corporation and Eastern Oil Transport in Wilmington, North Carolina, were our next acquisitions. Founded in 1950 by Eddie Cameron and Bill Bowen, this group was the distributor of Exxon fuel oils to industry in North Carolina and also operated a common-carrier, truck-tanker fleet. It had four truck terminals—in Wilmington, a 20-acre-track with waterfront on deep water on the Cape Fear River; Morehead City; Conway; and Selma. Its fleet consisted of 60 tractors and 120 trailers. It was the biggest independent distributor of fuel oil and the largest common-carrier of petroleum products in North Carolina and Virginia. Eddie Cameron, the former director of athletics at Duke University, became our Executive Vice President, and Bill Bowen continued as the General Operations Manager. Now we had waterfront property to build a terminal in Wilmington. Plus we had the legendary panache of Eddie Cameron to open doors for us—especially in North Carolina and with Duke fans everywhere. "Hello, Eddie Cameron and I would like to visit with you about your fuel oil requirements and also share his thoughts on the Blue Devils basketball season."

Another project to complete the logistics learned in "Boats" was the construction of the ocean tanker *Dolores Swann*. With 250,000-barrels of capacity, this ship, drawing 35 feet, was built at Saint John Shipbuilding & Dry Dock Company in Saint John, New Brunswick, Canada. Flying the flag of the Bahamas and with a Filipino crew, it made its maiden voyage in January 1978. This company-owned vessel joined the spot-charter tankers that we used every month.

With the logistics in place, the remaining concern was diversity in supply of the low-sulphur heavy oils. The Arab Embargo of 1973-1974 drove home the vulnerability of dependence on the Middle East. Swann Oil, with its multiple refinery suppliers, both domestic (Exxon, Shell, Gulf and Crown) and foreign (Agip, Sonotrack and CVP), had enough product to meet the demand of all our customers. Not one customer ran out of oil. In fact, we made emergency deliveries to customers assigned to us by the Federal Energy Administration. However, the 1973-1974 oil crisis caused us to scurry off the beaten path for small foreign refineries that were not dependent on Arab crude oil—small refineries in Africa, Sardinia, the Caribbean, Venezuela, Brazil and Mexico. I averaged 3000 air miles a week as I rushed to meet with Petróleo de Brasileiro S.A. (Petrobras) and Petróleos Mexicanos (Pemex) officials and secure term contracts to add to our existing contracts with Italy's Agip, Algeria's Sonotrack and Venezuela's CVP (in 1976 nationalized as Petróleos de Venezuela or PDVSA).

Our Pennsylvania Corporate Staff and Computer Department, consisting of 25 people, in 1975 were relocated to our newly purchased and renovated brick office buildings on Presidential Boulevard in Bala Cynwyd, about two blocks west of the boundary of Philadelphia. Dad's office and mine had panels of Brazilian Rose Wood, and all the furniture came from Knoll. The fabric of my desk chair was royal purple, my favorite color. Along one wall, I installed an eight-foot fish tank with rare and poisonous fish from the South Pacific. In the lobby was a large Harry Bertoia bronze sculpture created especially for us, which Bertoia named "Energy."

We also purchased a four-story office building next to our Presidential Boulevard property; this building was completely rented to third-party tenants.

To entertain our important industrial accounts and to reward our key employees, we contracted for private, sky boxes at the Vets Stadium and Spectrum Arena for Philadelphia Phillies, Eagles, 76ers and Flyers games and for celebrity concerts. Our Beechcraft King Air, which we purchased in 1975, flew in key customers for these events. I remember one baseball game when the Phillies' Phanatic parachuted into the stadium with the baseball to start the game, was blown by a gust of wind into the wall of the left-field bleachers, was hanging by his parachute with his leg broken, and the fans booed him for delaying the game and then clapped when the emergency ambulance drove from the field as Harry Kalas shouted "Outta Here!"

Even more memorable was the October 31, 1980, Phillies game at Vets Stadium with the lineup of Steve Carlton as the starting pitcher, Tug McGraw as the reliever, Bob Boone as catcher, Pete Rose at first base, Manny Trillo at second, Larry Bowa at short stop, Mike Schmidt at third, Greg Lazinski in left field, Gary Maddox in center field and "Shake and Bake" McBride in right field. The Phillies beat the Kansas City Royals, 4 to 1 in the sixth game of the World Series to win their first Championship in 98 years. And we caught a foul ball during that game.

By now my personal rolodex read like a "Who's Who" of the industrial leaders for most manufacturing facilities on the United States East Coast, including Clifford Goldsmith, President of Phillip Morris USA; Jack Guerin, Manager of Metropolitan Edison Company; Edward Henry, Vice president of Continental Can Company; Larry Marigold, Manager of Anheuser-Busch; Henry Nave, Chairman of Mack Trucks; and William Ogren, President of Alan Wood Steel. In addition, I knew the top executives at our two largest customers, Bethlehem Steel Corporation and Philadelphia Electric Company, which together purchased two million barrels of fuel oil each year from Swann Oil. Plus my rolodex included hundreds of independent domestic refinery officials, Greek ship-owners and export managers for refineries in Algeria, Sardinia, Italy, Venezuela, Brazil and Mexico.

My bulging rolodex, the memorable sporting events or the enticing shimmer of my poisonous fish did not blind me to my Sassamansville roots and the retail heating oil market, both residential and light commercial. We added three more tanks to the Sassamansville terminal to raise its storage capacity to 119,000 barrels (5 million gallons). The Atlantic Pipeline ran about 1/2 mile west of the terminal and could tie the Sassamansville tanks to our Schuylkill River terminal. So right of ways were purchased and our new pipeline connecting spur was under construction. When Dad grew tired of the State Highway Department's stalling on our permit applications to cross underneath Route 663 and Hoffmansville Road, Dad gathered his contractor buddies one weekend; tunneled under Route 663 near my infamous bologna sandwich culvert and under Hoffmansville Road near my old grade school; welded and installed the pipeline to complete the connection; and restored the landscaping. It's doubtful if any state bureaucrats ever knew our pipeline had been completed or that our Sassamansville terminal was connected to the three major pipeline systems that served the East Coast.

In 1977, Swann Oil bought the assets of Pennsylvania Independent Oil Company (Pennico) in Allentown for $1.2 million. Pennico owned 16 service stations, had 12 dealer-owned service stations, and more than 3,200 home heating oil customers. This Pennico business added to our existing Allentown home oil customer base, plus a small company that we also purchased west of Allentown, made Swann Oil the largest supplier of home heating oil in the Lehigh Valley. Add that to our Sassamansville customer base and Swann Oil had 15,000 heating oil customers—probably the largest number in Pennsylvania outside of metropolitan Philadelphia. The purchase of Pennico justified our hiring Mike Burke, a Harvard Business School graduate, as a Vice President to expand our service-station business and also to use his expertise with refineries in South America for additional supply of heavy fuel oils.

The score card at the end of the 1970's included five waterfront terminals in Pennsylvania, Virginia and Georgia; deep-water property in North Carolina; five inland terminals in Pennsylvania; four truck depots in North Carolina; 18 wholly-owned service stations in Pennsylvania; a combined tractor-trailer fleet of 500 tractors and 700 oil trailers; 60 tank-wagon trucks and 40 service vans and pickup trucks; a company-owned ocean tanker, three tugboats and three barges; two twin-engine airplanes; five corporate offices at Sassamansville, Allentown, Bala Cynwyd, New York City and Nassau, with a total property value of $63 million; about 700 employees; and annual sales approaching $400 million to 580 industrial accounts and 15,000 domestic customers.

With our business skyrocketing, Dad continued to oversee the truck transportation component in six maintenance facilities. As a pilot, he was directly involved in hiring our full-time pilots and particularly protective of our twin-engine Beechcraft King Air and Navajo airplanes, which were hangared at the Limerick Airport. But Dad's main passion became the construction, by Weller and Updegrove, of a 26-room mansion on a 10-acre tract in front of Grandpa's old farm property. Completed in 1977, Dad called it "The Swann Show House" to commemorate his parents. The Show House included rooms for his elaborate W3KLB Amateur Radio 1000-watt studio and his collection of vintage Gibson guitars and electric guitars. It had a night club (Dad's term) or a music room (Mother's term) in the basement, complete with a prewired sound system and fully-stocked, standard-sized bar with matching bar stools. Mother had a library with her dictionaries for her crossword puzzles. The adjacent four-car garage held the Cadillacs and Mercedes, plus had a suite for a private security guard. Dad also purchased a big shore house in Avalon, New Jersey (near Atlantic City) and a "snowbird" house in Miami Beach, Florida. Mother scurried to decorate and furnish their three new homes.

There was sadness when Grandma Brey died in May 1972, at age 86, with another hidden stash of Robitussin bottles. Harry Bertoia,

Dad's friend and sculptor, passed away in November 1978. ("He heard the voice of the wind, bringing sound from form to life.") Just two hours after Dad and Tres had visited with him, Uncle Vernon had a fatal heart attack in the shower in October 1979 at age 59. Having recently retired from active duty in the Air Force, Uncle Vernon probably was a victim of "when you rest, you rust." Uncle Russell, who received the Performing Fellowship from the Academy of Magical Arts in 1979, sadly died in March 1980, at age 78, alone in a small apartment in Scarsdale, New York, and was brought back to be the comedy magician buried in the Holy Cross Cemetery.

For the entire decade, I was frenetically gathering the components to create "Reverse Integration" and to maintain our reputation for dependable service while at the same time, balancing the persistent "P" factors—namely personnel recruitment, people problems, publicity, public service and personal life.

If an organization were to be greater than the sum of its people, attracting talented people was key to success. Of course, it started with family. David, after graduating with his Master's Degree from Lehigh University, built our computer department, managed the Allentown retail companies and then moved to Augusta to oversee the new terminal and marketing in that region.

Our first management employee hired a decade earlier, Mike Sanders, my Muhlenberg classmate, became a Vice President and managed the sales to industrial accounts in Pennsylvania. He had matured with our business philosophy based on service and reverse integration.

Jerry Batten, a graduate of Williamson, started as a supervisor of our Sassamansville terminal and advanced to Vice President of Operations for the entire company. His responsibilities also included all labor relations and negotiating our labor contracts. I never met a union boss or participated directly in a labor contract negotiation, because I remembered my history about President Woodrow Wilson directly negotiating at Versailles to end World War I and how his presence, as the ultimate decision-maker to include the formation of the League of Nations in the proposed Treaty of Versailles, trapped him in an uncompromising position that prevented the acceptance of that treaty by the U.S. Senate. I sent Jerry, without the authority to make a final commitment, so I would have time in a less emotional atmosphere to study any proposed agreement and counter with acceptable compromises.

Jack Tyrrell, a talented engineer with a Master's Degree from Villanova, joined us for the construction of the Schuylkill River terminal and then as Vice President of Engineering and Planning, managed the construction of every terminal, barge, tugboat and ship. His engineering skills were phenomenal.

A New York University graduate, John Stathis was our Vice President of Supply and Distribution and ran our 299 Park Avenue office in New York City. His primary responsibility was the spot purchase of fuels from overseas refineries. With his Greek heritage, he also negotiated our ship charters and handled our bunker fuel sales to ship owners or their agents, who frequently were fellow Greeks and had offices in New York. I spent many a late dinner at Athens by the Sea and Dionysos, popular Greek restaurants on New York's fashionable East Side, watching John and the ship owner's agent raise their restina and ouzo glasses as they haggled over a spot charter rate or the delivered price of bunker fuel. At one of these dinners, John made me an honorary Greek and gave me an icon of St. Iofunudi, the Greek patron saint of commerce.

An expert on domestic bulk supply was Thomas Gaffney. Coming to us from the Atlantic Refining Company, Tom became our Manager of Supply and Distribution with the task of buying domestic fuel oils and working arbitrages or exchanges with the domestic refineries to lower transportation costs. For example, we would deliver a cargo of Pemex heavy oil to an Exxon terminal in California and Exxon would repay us with an equal quantity of oil delivered to our Philadelphia terminal, thus our saving the freight differential.

Another expert in supply exchange was Ted Bishop, a former manager of Sinclair Refining Company. When brother David was elected to the Georgia House of Representatives, he was dividing his time between politics and the oil business. Then Ted Bishop was appointed President of Swann Oil Company of Georgia, oversaw our Savannah terminal, and handled exchanges, primarily with Sinclair. He set up the exchange for our delivering Pemex heavy oil with our shallow-draft tanker *Evgenia K. Chimples* to Sinclair's major utility customer in Florida and Sinclair's returning the equivalent product by barge from its Philadelphia refinery to our Schuylkill River terminal.

Again, we had the benefit of a major saving in freight and often received our product in advance of our re-delivery, thus a saving in interest costs for the time differential.

Our operation experts included Ed Gallagher, a licensed engineer, as the Operations Manager of our Philadelphia terminal; Tom Hitchcock, Muhlenberg Class of 1965, as Operations Manager of the Sassamansville terminal; and Ralph Bass, the new Operations Manager of the Chesapeake Terminal. A retired Army Master Sergeant, Ralph led his crew with "I expect an honest day's work for an honest day's pay." Mike Burke, Vice President, ran our service station venture. Al Munck kept our Marine Department afloat and had the responsibility for both our charter tankers and our wholly-owned *Dolores Swann*, three tugboats and three oil barges. From our Nassau, Bahamas office, Henry Hall supervised our foreign shipping corporation and also our offshore insurance company for more competitive access to the Lloyd's of London insurance market.

The best known member of our operations team was Eddie Cameron, the Executive Vice President of Eastern Oil Transport. Former athletic director of Duke University and member of the National College Football Hall of Fame, Eddie Cameron was an icon at Duke, where he was involved in Duke athletics from 1926 to 1972. Duke's basketball arena is named Cameron Indoor Stadium.

Heading our corporate Finance and Accounting Department was Gordon Tunstall, a graduate of Widener College and a Certified Public Accountant. That department included Jack Melchior as manager of Accounting; John Haffy as Credit Manager, who was the executive office employee with the most tenure after Mike Sanders; Tom Hitchcock as Purchasing Manager; Robert Kenney as Public Relations Manager; and Robert Lukens, a Harvard Law School graduate, as our in-house attorney for reviewing our financial agreements and contracts.

The most important non-family person on the team, from my perspective, was Janet Smith, my Administrative Assistant. Starting with my return from Drexel, Janet used her skills in shorthand and typing to capture my letters; managed my travel itinerary, which for many years averaged 3000 air miles per week; shielded me from the routine office hysteria; and even controlled my personal checkbook for paying all my personal bills. She was the real wizard behind the curtain.

My people skills—or lack thereof—were scrutinized in every interview. "Instead of relying on force of personality or just plain force," reported Ed Vilade in National Petroleum News, March 1973, "Leonard Swann relies on a rare quality—an intellect which can be brought to bear on practical matters, as well as abstract concepts." I told that reporter that I hired "a collection of aggressive prima donnas . . . All I want to be is Balanchine, the choreographer who gets them to dance to the same tune." What I really meant to say was "Every circus needs a ringmaster and in this circus it is I." Or to keep with my family name, I wanted swans, calm on the surface and paddling like hell below; or to follow Dad's advice, "Never, never let the S.O.B.'s know that you're hurting."

All the unusual people problems that crossed my radar had the verb "vanish" as the common denominator. After a tense renegotiation of a contract with the Teamsters Union in Philadelphia, which caused some of our company's profit to vanish, I purposely encouraged the hiring of Joan Khoshbin, a retired junior-high-school teacher, as a tractor-trailer driver. She became, with the mere hint of an "Equal Rights" challenge, the first female member of the Teamsters Union to drive a tractor-trailer in the Philadelphia area. The Evening Bulletin on May 23, 1974, featured a colored picture of her standing on a Swann Oil red-and-white tractor. The headline read: "She Traded Chalk for Truck." The article continued: "'What's this, women's lib?' queried another driver sarcastically. 'Not women's lib,' shot back Mrs. Khoshbin, a 5-foot-4 brunette. 'Just a woman trying to make an honest buck.'"

On a routine delivery to the Bethlehem Steel plant, a driver and his tractor-trailer completely vanished as if abducted by aliens. This impeccably-dressed driver, always in a starched and pressed uniform, was obsessively punctual on his delivery schedule. Days later, the loaded rig was found abandoned behind the Quakertown Diner on Route 309. The driver was located in the county jail. He had been arrested in an undercover sting for homosexual solicitation while taping his foot underneath the stall in the diner's bathroom. It gave the excuse "delayed by traffic" a new meaning.

About a year later, Harry, a burner service technician, and his service van vanished from the Allentown terminal. He had been arrested in drag, while soliciting at a truck stop. Imagine the burner service jokes that were told about that arrest—all beginning with "Call Dirty Harriet for service" and ending with "Dirty Harriet made my day."

A secretary at the Sassamansville office disappeared. Two weeks later, I received a post card from Germany, where she impulsively had rushed to marry her Army boyfriend. Al Purdenti, one of the first dispatchers hired at the Schuylkill River terminal, suddenly stopped coming to work. Several days later he called me and revealed—"My wife won $9 million in the New Jersey Lottery and I'm not letting her out of my sight."

Disconcerting was an emergency at the Allentown office. A bookkeeper passed out, was rushed by ambulance to the hospital and had emergency surgery to amputate gangrene toes from his left foot. The surgeon warned him to stop drinking cokes and smoking cigarettes, because they aggravated his diabetes and caused gangrene. "I would rather die than give up cokes and cigarettes," the bookkeeper replied. Two months later, they cut off his left foot; six months later, his left leg above the knee; and twelve months later, they buried what remained of him.

In 1978, the Virginia State Police arrested Leslie Beliles, the manager of our Chesapeake Terminal, three other terminal employees and six co-conspirators for stealing No.2 fuel oil, falsifying inventory records, hauling the stolen oil away in commandeered Swann trucks, and selling it for cash to a company in Moyock, North Carolina. They stole 518,000 gallons of fuel oil, worth $197,000. Beliles, who called himself "King of Currituck County," was sentenced to 29 years in prison with all but 29 months suspended. The others testified against Beliles and received suspended sentences.

A serious incident occurred in an African port, where our tanker *Dolores Swann* had called to load heavy oil. Because the refinery was upstream on a shallow channel, barges were used to transport the product to our ship anchored in the harbor. The captain had gone ashore and was arrested by a rival tribal chief, who demanded the payment of a "fine" of $200,000 in American currency. A local lawyer and diplomat delivered the cash to pay the ransom and escorted the captain back to our ship.

Publicity during the period 1973-1976 was unbelievable. There were 13 articles in regional and national publications on Swann Oil; examples of the typical titles follow: "The Next Leon Hess?

Leonard Swann 'Integrating Back'—toward Major Level" in <u>National Petroleum News</u>, March 1973; "Swann Oil . . . A Company Integrating Backwards" in <u>Delaware Valley Industry</u>, May 1973; "Swann Oil . . . A Quarter Century of Growth Through Service" in <u>The Philadelphia Purchasor</u>, September 1973; "Turned down by Philadelphia banks, Swann Oil made it big anyway" in <u>Focus: Philadelphia's Independent Business Newsweekly</u>, May 28, 1975; "An oil independent that hit it right" in <u>Business Week</u>, June 2, 1975; "Local banks refuse to loan to local business" in <u>The Sunday Bulletin</u>, June 13, 1975; and "Petroleum Transportation Tailored to the Needs of Tar heel Industry" in <u>North Carolina Magazine</u>, July 1976.

An article "From Country Boy to Oil Magnate" in <u>Destination Philadelphia</u>, July 1976, quoted Dad. "My philosophy was just to work a little harder than anyone else," Dad said. "I can still remember delivering fuel oil six days a week. Then, on Sunday after Church, I'd work on the truck to get it ready for the next week's deliveries." To which I added: "The expansion of our company has been based on the primary philosophy established by the founder of the company: find the need of the ultimate user of fuel oil and then take all the necessary steps to satisfy it . . . We have reversed the process . . . integrating backwards."

My Brother David had come up with the marketing slogan "You can't call Mr. Exxon . . . but you can call David Swann," which the business reporters amended to include calling me. With my tight schedule, I tried to be responsive for the sake of the free publicity but I really wanted to restrict my publicity efforts to key speaking engagements. I gave the keynote speech—"The History of Swann Oil and current assessment of World-Wide Energy Situation"—in August 1976 to the Americans for the Competitive Enterprise System regional meeting in Reading. In 1979, at the Albright College Alumnae Luncheon in Reading, I delivered my analysis on "The Energy Crisis and National Energy Policy." Phillip Morris invited me to speak at its 1980 Financial Conference at Marco Island, Florida. My speech was entitled "Energy Strategies for the 1980's." My academic interests were evident in several lectures on "The American Clyde, The Preeminence of the Delaware River in Shipbuilding After the Civil War" and "John Roach, Shipbuilding Entrepreneur" at the Philadelphia Maritime Museum.

Public service activities included my participation in the growth of the Philadelphia Maritime Museum, founded by J. Welles Henderson, one of our corporate attorneys; the occasional talk to Phi Alpha Theta at Muhlenberg College; four years ending in 1975 as a Trustee of the Montgomery County Community College; a member of the Board of Directors at the Agnes Irwin School in Rosemont, where Heather began her formal education; and a member of the Parents' Committee for Portsmouth Abbey School, the boarding school in Rhode Island that Paul attended. My public service interest was education but my discretionary time was limited.

Addressing these "P" factors provided momentary distractions from my roller coaster ride with Dolores. When we were traveling abroad on my business trips, our relationship was a story book romance. She was happy and supportive. We flew to Rome, where I negotiated a supply contract for low-sulphur heavy oil; then we prayed at St. Peter's Cathedral and the Sistine Chapel, stared at the Coliseum and threw three coins in Trevi Fountain. We traveled to London, where Brian Graves introduced me to his colleagues in Lloyd's of London; then Dolores and I watched the Changing of the Guard at Buckingham Palace, paid homage to Vice Admiral Horatio Nelson and the HMS *Victory*, visited the site of the rebuilt Globe Theatre and traveled to Shakespeare's house at Stratford-on-Avon. We jetted to Paris, where I negotiated with Banque Paribas; then we saw the Mona Lisa and the Last Supper at the Louvre and climbed the Eiffel Tower. On one trip to Athens, after my exploring with George Chimples the renewing of the term charter on his tanker, we were mesmerized by the Parthenon. We returned to Rio de Janeira, where I met with Petrobras to work out the details for another oil contract; then we revisited Ipanema Beach where we relived our euphoric engagement days. We flew to Mexico City and stayed at the Camino Real Hotel. I negotiated a major contract with Pemex. Dolores used her Spanish to regale Roberto Osegueda, the Pemex Manager of Foreign Commerce, and his wife at dinner; and I showed off my Spanish—"La cuenta, por favor." And so it went. When we were on the international air routes and living the life of wealthy connoisseurs, our relationship was magical.

But when we returned to Villanova and our children, there was a bipolar regression. Dolores was agitated, argumentative and aggressive all the time. It got so bad that the children and I developed a code for

"Getting out of Dodge" when Dolores was on a rampage. The code was "Donut Time." We'd run to my car and head to a small donut shop in Conshocken for chocolate-covered, custard-filled donuts. We had "Donut Time" so often that the shop owner would already be filling our order as we walked into his bakery.

Often after a tirade, Dolores needed shopping therapy. She would rush out to Lord and Taylor, her favorite Department Store, and buy indiscriminately and charge willy-nilly. After one argument, Dolores charged a super-expensive sofa, which cost about two years of school tuition at Agnes Irwin School. That "I'll-show-you" sofa wound up in the sun room.

Dolores micromanaged every aspect of our children's education. She felt that Episcopal Academy was not challenging enough for Paul; so in September 1970, Paul entered Portsmouth Abbey School, Portsmouth, Rhode Island. Founded in 1926 by the Benedictine monks, this strict boarding school averaged 225 students in grades 8 through 12 and sent about two dozen graduates a year to Ivy League Colleges. Dolores oversaw every course and was especially concerned if Paul participated in athletic activities during the academic year. With my serving on the Parents' Committee influencing the school's recommendation and with additional push from a recommendation letter from Professor Freidel, Paul entered Harvard in 1974 and, after graduation in 1978, wanted to attend law school. I contacted Eddie Cameron, my current Executive Vice President of Eastern Oil Transport in North Carolina. The legendary Eddie Cameron, the former director of athletics at Duke University, secured an admission for Paul to start the 1978 fall semester at Duke Law School.

Heather began grade school, fall 1972, at the Agnes Irwin School in Rosemont. Again Dolores hovered over every aspect of Heather's studies at this grade school; and I had discreet oversight as a member of the school's Board of Directors. But at the end of fourth grade, Dolores threatened to sue Agnes Irwin because the school's guidance counselor had administered I.Q. tests to Heather without permission from Dolores and had recorded the scores in Heather's general files. Dolores also claimed that the tests were incorrectly graded and that Heather's score was too low, because it was only in the low-genius range. Heather was yanked from the school at Christmas 1977 and sent to The Baldwin

School in Bryn Mahr. Totally embarrassed, I resigned from the Agnes Irwin board.

At The Baldwin School, with its mission "From Thinking Girls to Accomplished Women," Heather had a course in ballroom dancing. For her first date ever, J.B. Dillsheimer III, wearing a tuxedo, was chauffeured by his parents to escort Heather to a Cotillion at which no parents were allowed. I stared at J.B. Dillsheimer III as he left our house. I picked up Dad and we rushed to the auditorium, used an Andrew Jackson to encourage a janitor to open a rear door for us, climbed up in the balcony, hid behind the railing and spied on the dancers. "Dad, did you see that?" I whispered. "That jerk J.B. just slid his hand down Heather's back." Dad's retort was: "What do you expect? He is the son of one of those Philadelphia bankers who turned down our terminal loan." Heather later told me she punched J.B. when he attempted to kiss her in the car.

Even Tres was not immune from Dolores' total supervision. Tres started kindergarten at the Haverford School in September 1975. Founded in 1884, Haverford was considered to be the best all boys preparatory school in the greater Philadelphia area. After an argument over the quality of the Mathematics Program in third grade, Dolores yanked Tres from Haverford in March 1979 and enrolled him in mid-term at the Rosemont School of the Holy Child, a Catholic school conducted by the Society of the Holy Child Jesus, founded by Cornelia Connelly in 1846. Almost immediately, there were so many complaints by Dolores on the stupidity of the teaching nuns that I was constantly visiting Sister Helen McDonald, head of the school, to defuse the tension. After every blow up, Sister Helen had tea and cookies ready for my anticipated visit to find a resolution. Sister Helen's father and my Dad died within months of each other. Sister Helen, with her religious perspective, was very helpful with my grief, and I reciprocated by listening to her reminiscences about her father.

Tres made the Fifth grade football team as a running back. At one game against Norwood School, the linebacker, who had a plaster cast on his arm, kept whacking Tres on the helmet with his cast, often after the play had ended. His father was pacing the side lines and yelling, "Hit him again, harder!" I muttered to myself—"Jesus, if that kid whacks Tres again, I'm going to take both him and his G.D. father out." From behind me came an angelic voice. "I think Jesus has more important things to consider," said Sister Helen. "But, I agree with your plan."

Our children's education followed the pattern of explosion, resolution and donation—Dolores' irrational explosions, my missions of resolution to defuse the crises, and then my donations to the school library funds. I averaged $4,000 a year in donations to the libraries at the various schools.

An irrational litigation gene was part of Dolores' personality. It was exhibited in her threats of law suits against Agnes Irwin School, against her sister over some furniture from her mother's estate, and often against merchants. On one trip to Cambridge, Dolores purchased a pocketbook for $300 from a boutique near Harvard Square. The handle clasp broke. The merchant offered to fix it but Dolores wanted a full refund. The merchant refused. Dolores hired a prominent Boston law firm and spent $4,600 in legal fees to sue the store in order to force a refund of $300. She needed to win at any cost, rather than spend the same amount for 15 new pocketbooks or reallocate it to cover a part of the tuition expenses for Heather and Tres or the Annual Library Fund. But the money was not coming out of her pocket.

At Villanova, in 1977, we doubled the size of our house by adding five more rooms, (including a large indoor garden room that could double as a ballroom), another two-car garage and a large, indoor swimming pool with a separate whirlpool and sauna. The sliding glass roof over the pool was an architectural marvel. Constructed around the entire property was a high brick and metal fence with an electric gate.

To fulfill another of Dolores' dreams—a summer house at Cape Cod—I built that summer house in Wellfleet, Massachussetts, overlooking the bay. After a local contractor erected the shell, Weller and Updegrove finished the interior; and Bill Berkey, the plumbing and heating. Dolores, the children, house keeper and dogs stayed there every summer. I flew in on our company Beechcraft King Air on weekends; often traded two bottles of Scotch with my regular cab driver, who was a lobsterman during the week, for two bushel-baskets of clams and lobsters; and prepared a New England Clam Bake for Saturday dinner. Also, we had dinner often with the Freidels, who owned a cottage a few blocks from us.

One Saturday, Dolores' cousin and his family were visiting from Brockton. After our Clam Bake dinner, we began playing nickel-and-dime poker. An argument erupted between Dolores and her cousin over the limit for each raise—could it be more than a dime? Dolores started screaming and swept the cards and coins off the table. Her cousin shouted back that Dolores was a cheat and thief, just like her grandfather in Zahlé, who, years ago, had moved the rocks that delineated the boundaries of the garden patches to steal land from his relatives. Her cousin packed his family in their car and yelled as he drove off: "You're a cheating Ackel bitch!" I was dumbfounded that an old, foreign family feud over a few feet of garden in Zahlé had resurfaced in Wellfleet.

The following New Year's Eve, we continued our custom of attending a black-tie dinner at Alma and Jack Coggins farm, west of Sassamansville. The country literati congregated, confabulated, congratulated and celebrated the coming of the New Year. Arriving home after 3 AM, I was slow in opening the passenger door for Dolores. She let loose with a maniacal rage, rushed up to our bedroom and locked the door. For the next six weeks, she did not talk to me, and I slept in the family room in the basement. Then, one day, Dolores asked—as if nothing had happened—why was I sleeping in the basement and ignoring her?

Like a horror film, Dolores' paranoid, bipolar eruptions led to the disintegration of my romantic illusions, raised my concern that I had been duped by this older woman (whose actions fit the definition of a "Cougar," a new term in popular psychology to describe an older woman who preys on a younger man through marriage), magnified my self-pity for being taken for granted, encouraged my scheduling as many solo business trips as possible, and confronted me with the possibility of a sterile, isolated future. Where would this high-budget horror film end?

Picture Days

Grandparents Swann, 50th Wedding Anniversary on the
porch of the farmhouse (1947).

Uncle Russell,
the magician, entertaining
Rita Hayworth.

Mother   Dad

Dad playing guitar at the farm (1938).

Uncle Vernon in the Army Air Force.

Uncles Dick and Vernon (1939).   Uncle Dick in the Marine Corps.

Grandparents Swann, 50th Wedding Anniversary Celebration (1947).
Back row from the left: Dad, Aunt Sarah, Uncles Sidney, Preston and Jack.
Middle row from the left: Mother, Mr. Kappas, Aunt Helen, Grandpa, Grandma, Aunts Louise and Lou, Uncle Vernon.
Front row from the left: Cousins Charlotte and Ruth, Brother David, Cousin Karen.

Father Leo J. Letterhouse is at bottom right. Aunt Helen is at top left.

Standing from left: Uncles Dick, Vernon, Russell; Dad and Uncle Sidney.
Sitting from left: Uncles Jack and Joe.

I am the infant in Mother's arms,
the First Age of William Shakespeare's Seven Ages of Man (1939).

Mother and me.

Dad (1943)   Mother, cute David and me.

Dad was a radioman on the GP-16.

David, Grandma Brey and me (1944).

Hickory Park Restaurant.

Hoffmansville School.

Dad and Mother.   Mother (1945).

On left, Grandma Brey at the tour   My Second Grade photo.
bus for the Hyde Park trip (1947).

I am the School Boy, the Second Age of Shakespeare's
Seven Ages of Man (1946).

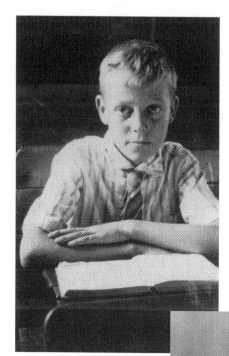

Dad, age 11 at
Hoffmansville
School (1929).

My Fourth Grade
at Hoffmansville
School (1948).

My Fifth Grade at Perkiomenville School—
Hey, it's my memoir (1949).

David and I pose
in Uncle Jim's
carnival scene.

Uncle Jack with his
"you better do the
right thing" stare.

Dad and Mother at the Visitation Blessed Virgin Mary
Catholic Church in Green Lane.

Judy Horne is
"Depression" and
I am "John Alden" in
One Mad Night at High
School (1954).

My Senior photo in the Walum
Olum hints of my Lover status,
the Third Age in Shakespeare's
Seven Ages of Man (1955).

Dad, Mother, David and me.

Mother at my Graduation from Muhlenberg College.

My Graduation from Muhlenberg College (June 7, 1959).

Uncle Jack at my Graduation.

John Roach, my second entrepreneurial idol.

Mother and Dad on vacation in Atlantic City, NJ.

Rachael, Debby and I visit Zoo New England.

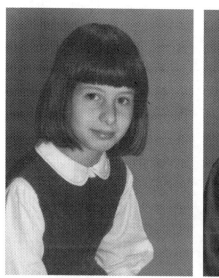

Debby.   Rachael.

My Graduation from Harvard,
with Mother and Dad
(June 13, 1963).

Dad's second L.A. Swann tank-wagon truck.

Dad's first oil terminal (1951).

Dad in the first company office.

Dad's first truck garage and office (1951).

Dad and his Cessna.

Dad in his first private office of Swann Oil, Inc.,
across the highway from his first truck garage.

Mother and Dad in the lobby of the new Swann Oil office (1972).

Uncle Jack,
Captain in the PA State Police.

David, the company's computer guru (1972).

I am the President of Swann Oil, Inc. (1972).

Swann Oil's Schuylkill River Terminal.

The *Evgenia K. Chimples* makes its first delivery of heavy fuel oil
to the Schuylkill River Terminal (July 11, 1973).

Dad in the radio room of the *Evgenia K. Chimples.*

I am standing on the deck of the *Evgenia K. Chimples* with, from the left, the Captain, David, Tres, Mike Sanders and Dad.

Tres and I visit the wheelhouse of the *Evgenia K. Chimples.*

Mother and Dad at the christening of the *Marie Swann* at
Savannah, GA (May 22, 1975).

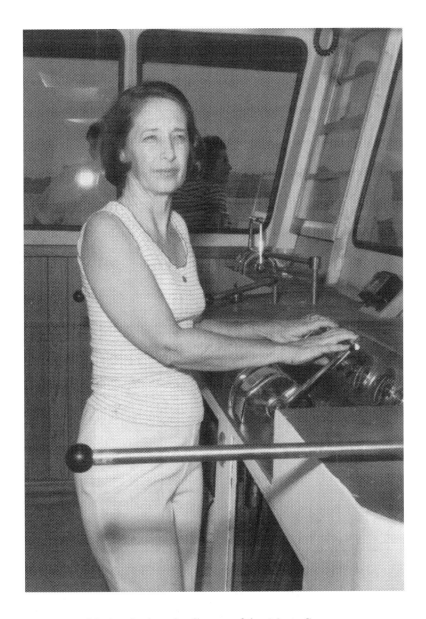

Mother in the wheelhouse of the *Marie Swann*.

The Swann Oil Chesapeake, VA Terminal.

David's campaign card for the
Georgia House of Representatives.

Grandma Brey—
"Don't be fussin' with my 'tussin."

Dad in the music room of the Swann Show house.

In our Bala Cynwyd, PA, office, I am the President of Swann Oil, the
Energetic Soldier, the Fourth Age of Shakespeare's
Seven Ages of Man (1978).

Dad with Chet Atkins in New York City (1979).

My last picture of Mother and Dad together (1980).

Tres.   Heather.

Heather on Liseter Fancy Dragon.

I am standing with Gayle and Tres beside the 315-pound Blue Marlin
caught by Gayle off Oregon Inlet (July 1984).

I am with Mother and Tres (1985).

Tres, the drummer (1987)

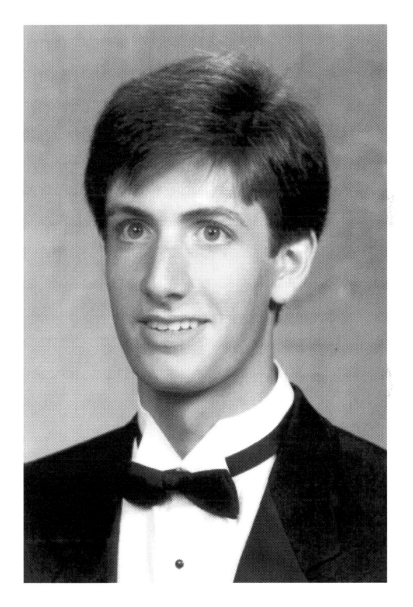

Tres' Senior Picture at Norfolk Academy (1988).

Ari, Jacquelyn and Jennifer.

Uncles Joe, Dick and Jack at Uncle Dick's Ordination
as Deacon in the Catholic Church (September 13, 1986).

I am the besieged with "eyes severe,"
the Fifth Age in Shakespeare's Seven Ages of Man (late 1980's).

Leonard A. Swann, Jr.

Shadow's Sassylass
of Scotchhill,
a.k.a. Sassy.

Gayle and I attend Jennifer's Wedding (1990).

The TFC Band front men (1991).

Gayle and I edit the TFC video,
the first release by Sirocco Productions (1991).

On the Caribbean Cruise Ship *Sunward II,* Gayle and I are dressed for the Banquet to receive the Award for Highest Blastrac Sales.

Gayle and I attend Tres' Graduation from William and Mary College (1992).

Gayle and I host Robin Woods, doll artist.

Gayle and I are married in Las Vegas (July 27, 1996).

Leonard A. Swann, Jr.

Tres, Deborah, Rachael and I attend
a Swann Family Reunion at Williamsburg, VA.

I escort Heather down the aisle (1996).

My "never, never let the S.O.B's know that you're hurting" posture.

My last photo of Mother, with her great-granddaughter.

Gayle and I receive "Who's Who" Awards
at the Madame Alexander Doll Club's Convention (1997).

Seated from the left, Anne Rice and Gayle;
Standing from the left, Peter Coe, Paul Crees and me (1999).

Seated third from left is Gayle at the Hitty Banquet, where the Hittites
traded pajamas for red hats. I am smiling when I think
about the things I did for videos!

Gayle—
can you see now how I survived for the last three decades?

Gayle and I visit the bull at Billie Bob's Honky Tonk.

Gayle.

Gayle and I enjoy the beach,
where I philosophize about waves, tides and sand crabs (2008).

The *George H.W. Bush*—Specialty Products performed the shotblasting of the flight deck (2008).

I'm with "spectacles ... and pouch,"
the Sixth Age of Shakespeare's Seven Ages of Man,
and working to avoid the last Age of "second childishness
and mere oblivion" (2011).

Disintegration Days

There I was, on June 1, 1978, in a state of shock in the waiting room of Pottstown Medical Center, having just been informed by a surgeon that Dad had cancer of the liver which had metastasized to reduce his life expectancy to about two months.

How could this be true? Dad was barely 60 years old. Since World War II, Dad had been to the hospital only once—in 1958 for emergency surgery to remove kidney stones. He felt so healthy that he refused to have periodic physicals. Then yesterday on the way to their shore house at Avalon, New Jersey, he had blacked out at the Delaware River toll booth. Mother rushed him to the Pottstown Medical Center. Dr. Charles Delp, the family doctor, diagnosed an obstruction in the carotid artery and scheduled an endarterectomy. Blood tests for the surgery revealed the cancer cells. I should have suspected that something was wrong when Mother and I had been waiting six hours before any doctor came out to update us.

Mother was hysterical, ranging from denial to anger, especially when Dr. Delp gave his realistic but disheartening prognosis that all treatment options were palliative not curative. When Mother went to visit Dad in the recovery room, I called Dolores. "Dad has cancer of the liver and only a few months to live," I blurted out through choking sobs. "We can talk about it later," Dolores shouted. "You're late! You know that we are hosting a dinner for the Schlesinger Library. Arthur Schlesinger is on his way from the airport. Ruth Seltzer of the Philadelphia Inquirer is due here any minute. You're late! Get home immediately!"

"But Dolores," I muttered, "didn't you hear me? Dad is dying!" Dolores screamed—"I don't care. Get home now! We'll discuss it later." I hung up the phone. And for the second time in my life, I threw my emotional switch to "off." The details of the separation and the divorce could be worked out after Dad passed away.

Somehow I made the dinner, muddled through the fund raising event for the Arthur and Elizabeth Schlesinger Library on the History of Women in America at Radcliffe College, and chatted with the Schlesingers, Friedels, Horners, Biddles, Campbells, Clothiers, Smiths, Coggins, and dozens of others. But inwardly I was devastated. Dolores got her write up in the social page of the <u>Philadelphia Inquirer</u> but not as the lead article and two months later was appointed to the Advisory Board of the Schlesinger Library. She gained a board seat but was losing a husband.

I had no Father Letterhouse to consult so I turned to Uncle Joe. "Unlike a heart attack," he pointed out, "cancer gives you a warning and time to say and do the things you usually put off doing." Uncle Joe concluded, "Spend time with your Dad and let him know how much you love him and respect what he has done."

Our Virginia bankers invited Dolores and me to the black-tie Governor's Dinner in Norfolk in July. Coincidentally, Heather was riding in a horse show in Virginia Beach on the next day. Two days before the scheduled events, Dolores' German Shepherd became ill; the local veterinarian suspected kidney malfunction due to cancer. For this cancer victim, Dolores immediately tracked down a veterinary specialist in Mobile, Alabama, commandeered our Beechcraft King Air to fly her and the dog to Mobile and left the children and me high and dry. I called Ralph Bass, Manager of the Chesapeake Terminal, for help with a babysitter for Heather and Tres at the Omni Hotel while I attended the Governor's Dinner. Ralph asked his office assistant, Gayle Dunn O'Neal. Lightning struck when I chatted with her after the formal dinner. Although she was separated from her husband and was supporting three children, she had an infectious smile and radiated positive energy. Moreover, she was a younger, more beautiful version of my Mother—kind, intelligent, energetic, hardworking, self-sufficient—and a walking endorsement for Dad's mantra "Never let the bastards get you down." I immediately fell in love with her. As Shakespeare wrote, "Whoever loved that loved not at first sight."

Margaret Gayle Dunn was born on January 2, 1947, with an Irish and French Huguenot heritage. Sadly, her mother, Margaret Emma Smith, a registered nurse, had died in 1964, at the age of 46, from cancer. Her father, Clifford Dozier Dunn, a superintendent at Charles W. Priddy Fertilizer Company, had died in 1969, at the age of 56, from a heart attack. Gayle was the only girl in a pack of four brothers and one half-brother. After high school, she held full-time jobs as a switchboard operator and secretary to support her family of twin daughters and a son. She had me from the first look into her magical brown eyes.

For our first date, we went to the Naro Theater in Norfolk for the rerelease of the classic <u>Gone With The Wind</u>, starring Vivien Leigh and Clark Gable. As I sat there captive for four hours, meeting Scarlett O'Hara and Rhett Butler for the first time, soaking up antebellum Southern Culture, and waiting and waiting for the action-packed Civil War battle scene which never appeared on the screen, I suspected that Southerners were in a time warp, that I would starve to death, and that my plans for the evening were derailed. "Frankly, my dear" . . ."As God is my witness, I'll never be hungry again" . . ."I'll think about that tomorrow."

The second weekend in August, I introduced Gayle to Dad when we took him to the 43rd annual Fiddler's Convention in Galax, Virginia, which was the oldest and largest old-time fiddler's convention in the world. For three days, fiddles, guitars and banjos playing "Old Joe Clark" . . ."Black Mountain Rag" . . ."Bile Them Cabbage Down" . . ."John Henry" and other traditional country and mountain songs echoed from the stage and the tailgating bands rehearsing in the parking lot. When I closed my eyes, I was back in my parents' secure basement. This fiddler's convention sealed my commitment to Gayle, because during a break in the music, Dad whispered in my ear "She's a keeper!"

Next it was my turn to be vetted. Gayle arranged for a meeting with her four brothers at the bar of the Omni Hotel in Norfolk. Gathered there were Cliff, a recently retired Marine harrier pilot with 25 years of service; Frank, with one tour of duty in the Air Force and now the owner of a supply company for military parts; Rick, with one tour of duty in the Marines and now a firefighter; and W.T., with one tour of duty in the Marines and now owner of a pizza shop. They averaged 5-feet, 7-inches in height, and together they had 12 marriages. They immediately began tossing back Jamison's Irish Whiskey on the rocks—all on my tab—and kept asking me, almost like a chorus, "Are your intentions honorable?" There I was 6-feet tall and a teetotaler, since I had stopped drinking the occasional Dubonet and the infrequent ouzo as one of the promises in my bargain with God to help Dad through his cancer. "I hope to marry Gayle if she will have me when we can legally do it," was my presumptuous answer. Next I had to endure the family initiation rite. After each placing $20 on the center of the table—including Gayle's $20—sleeves on both arms were rolled up and we began an elimination Arm Wrestling Match, first with the right arm and next with the left. Where was Uncle Sidney when I needed him? Hours later, with two sore arms and hundreds of dollars poorer, I was welcomed into the Dunn Clan.

Frantic activity became my denial and coping mechanism. I accompanied Dad to every chemotherapy and radiation treatment, then took him to his favorite restaurant in Pennsburg for lunch and sat with him as he curled in a tiger blanket on the sofa at home until his nausea subsided. Johns Hopkins Hospital in Baltimore offered an experimental therapy for liver cancer. I got Dad included in the program and drove him to each session. I planned trips for Dad—to another Old Fiddler's Convention in Galax, two weeks of vacation in Mexico City with Mother and my family, a trip to a Chet Atkins concert in New York City, where I arranged for Chet Atkins to meet privately with Dad, Janet Smith and Bill Berkey in his hotel suite and play guitar duos with Dad.

As my estrangement and arguments with Dolores increased, I often slept on the couch in my Bala Cynwd office, where luckily there was a bathroom and shower. In preparation for leaving Villanova, I purchased Grandpa's old farm house and the 23 acres remaining from the family farm near Sassamansville—which Uncle Joe talked the absentee owner into selling—for my Pennsylvania refuge and parked a new DeLorean there. Next, I gave up my apartment lease at the Hague Towers and purchased a new town house on Botetourt Street in Norfolk for my southern refuge and parked a Mercedes hardtop there. I also bought building lots in Virginia Beach and Nags Head, North Carolina.

To distract myself from Dad's lingering fatal illness and Dolores' constant harassment, I created a flurry of business enterprises and acquisitions, all focused in the South. I organized Lynnhaven Launch Services. It operated from a dock and marina on Lynnhaven Bay, and ran seven launches as water taxis to ferry crew members and supplies to the container ships and coal ships anchored in the Chesapeake Bay, waiting for dock space to load. Hampton Roads was the largest coal exporting port in the world. There were usually a dozen coal ships waiting to load but with periodic coal strikes in Poland, there were sometimes as many as 100 coal ships waiting in the Chesapeake Bay. Lynnhaven Launch Services also owned a water barge to supply fresh water to these ships and spot chartered our tug *Maggie Swann* (named after my Grandma Maggie Brey) to tow the water barge. The seven Lynnhaven launches, the water barge, dock and marina cost $2.1 million.

Cygnet Communications Company, with an investment of $3.1 million, was my intellectual distraction. It published monthly regional magazines. The first acquisition in 1980 was Commonwealth, a magazine founded in 1934 by the Virginia Chamber of Commerce, followed by purchases of Norfolk's Metro magazine, Richmond's Lifestyle magazine and Charlottesville's Albermarle magazine, which were merged into Commonwealth to raise its paid monthly circulation to about 48,000 copies. Also, North Carolina's Tar Heel and South Carolina's Sandlapper were acquired and merged into Carolina Lifestyle, the regional magazine for North Carolina and South Carolina, with a paid monthly circulation of 36,000 copies. Published also were an inflight magazine for Altair airlines, Altair Away, and tourist Guidebooks for Richmond and Tidewater Virginia.

To house the magazine staff, there were rental offices in Richmond, Virginia, and Raleigh, North Carolina; in addition, a historic building at Blanding Street in Columbia, South Carolina, and a three-story building at College Place in Norfolk were purchased. The College Place building was remodeled. The top floor became my citadel; it had my executive office with a fireplace, my private bathroom with shower, an admin office, a conference room, my private dining room with kitchen and hand-made china that incorporated the Cygnet Logo, and a rose garden on the roof-top patio adjacent to the glass wall of my office. My interest in growing roses, which I inherited from Mother, was a pleasant hobby. From this citadel, not only could I function as publisher of the magazines, but also as the executive over Swann Oil enterprises which totaled 26 companies and my personally-owned southern companies which totaled 16.

"What kind of man would . . . insist that his executive chair be royal purple?" queried John McManus in an article, "Uncovering the Man behind the magazines," in Norfolk's The Ledger Star on February 17, 1982. "Or keep a tank of rare poisonous tropical fish in the suite of his suburban Philadelphia headquarters? Or be regarded by almost all who meet him as brilliant, if eccentric? . . . Leonard Swann is such a man . . . most recently, Leonard Swann has gotten into publishing . . . in a big way and with an eye to buying all competitors."

The article went on to describe me—"He's sort of a mystery man . . . highly intelligent . . . a very tough man to deal with . . . very aggressive . . . a dictator . . . obsessed with privacy . . . frightening . . . demands total control of all he touches . . . aloof . . . tough." But one anonymous woman who was interviewed found me "very charming!"

Next, I purchased Virginia Materials in Norfolk for $2.4 million. Virginia Materials had a manufacturing plant that refined a special coal slag, brought in by railcar from Ohio Power Company's electric generating plants, to produce a Black Blast Abrasive. This blasting abrasive, delivered in bulk by the company's special pump trailers or in 5-ton metal bins, was used by the shipyards in Tidewater Virginia to prepare ship hulls and decks for painting. My plan was to upgrade the plant to produce a second product—a proprietary roofing granule additive for the manufacturing of roofing shingles—which I had already contracted to supply to Certainteed, a large producer of shingles.

For Paul Ernest, Heather and Tres, I had established irrevocable Trusts in 1975 to cover their college educations. Now to support Heather's interest in competitive amateur riding in national horse shows, I set up another Trust in 1979 for Heather and built an equestrian center on 10 acres of prime land at Darby Paoli Road, Berwyn, Pennsylvania. I invested $500,000 in that property with a farm house and the construction of a 19-stable horse barn with an attached indoor show arena and an outdoor show ring, which was named Ashley Meadows Farm. Also, I bought Heather show ponies and horses, including "Liseter Fancy Dragon" . . ."Ice Castles" . . . and "Why Not Julie," a blue ribbon horse that cost $150,000. Heather rode Ice Castles and Why Not Julie in 1982, 1983, and 1984 in the Madison Square Garden Horse Show, the premier event in the National Horse Show Circuit. Also, Heather, her mother, a full-time private trainer and trailer driver spent six weeks every winter on the Florida Horse Show Circuit to earn points for the national competition.

Dolores had added show ponies and show horses to her dog obsession. She wanted to be recognized in the National Horse Show Circuit alongside the Duponts; to be a celebrity with her own box at the annual Devon Horse Show, one of the most visible social events on the Philadelphia Main Line; and to show up the old Main Line Bluebloods. Ashley Meadows Farm and Heather were Dolores' trump cards. She became obsessed with Heather's riding performance at horse shows. At one event, Heather's timing was off and her horse missed a jump. When Heather exited the ring, Dolores screamed at Heather, pulled her from the saddle and beat her with a riding crop in front of incredulous bystanders. I intervened to protect Heather; and I never went to another horse show.

Insensitive to Dad's physical decline, disgusted with my frantic coping distractions and my throwing money left and right, the myopic and paranoid Dolores was harassing me constantly. She hired a private detective, who uncovered my purchases of Grandpa's farm house and the Botetourt Street town house and my relationship with Gayle. For days, he parked near my town house, snapped photographs and followed me. Dolores ranted at me—in her descending order of importance—for not being more supportive of her involvement with the American Horse Show Association and Heather's horse show aspirations; for my secret finances and purchases of real estate and magazines; for my obsessive involvement with Dad's cancer treatments; for luring her from Boston College and then isolating, ignoring and abandoning her in Villanova; for not being a good Catholic but a hypocrite attending Mass on Sundays; for having a "hoity-toity midlife crisis like the hoi polloi"; for being a "narcissist and evil incarnate"; and finally for my infidelity.

I secretly began consulting a psychiatrist, on a biweekly basis, in New York City. After ten sessions, he concluded that my delay in officially separating from Dolores was reprehensible since that relationship was dead. "You are a wimp for not leaving." He evaluated my new relationship with Gayle as caring, loving and committed with a high probability for a successful marriage—particularly since she reminded me of my Mother. Marriage to Gayle would restore my self-esteem, enhance my sense of self-worth and support my desire to be "good"—a good son, good husband, good father and good Catholic. It would be a new positive experience, the psychiatrist concluded. I had stumbled on a psychiatrist who could interpret the positive results of a benign Oedipus complex. I thought of my Mother's country advice—"Quit while you're ahead. Shut up and leave before you talk yourself into a hole."

Dad miraculously and bravely struggled for three years, losing about 120 pounds and eventually sinking into the depth of despair. Surrounded by his family, he died on August 2, 1981, in Pottstown Medical Center. It was the saddest day of my life and marked the beginning of the collapse of my world. I lost my idol, my mentor, my protector and my best friend.

At the visitation at Mann Funeral Home in East Greenville, 337 mourners attended—including his old friends John Bauman and Tom Strong—and 148 floral tributes were displayed. I was especially sad that Gayle did not attend to pay her last respects to Dad and support me in this sad period. After a Requiem Mass, Dad was interred in the new family mausoleum that I had built at the Holy Cross Cemetery in Pennsburg. On that day, Swann Oil tractor-trailers made over 400 deliveries of fuel oil to industrial customers located in the region from Philadelphia to Savannah. It was an appropriate salute to my Dad, who loved the truck hustle and who promised timely service to the very end.

That night Mother offered me the pick of Dad's possessions. The only item I wanted, accepted and treasured was his protective tiger blanket.

There was an estrangement with my brother David over the strategic direction of the petroleum enterprise and the decision not to pursue its sale to Sun Oil Company or Gulf Oil Company. Both had expressed an interest in purchasing Swann Oil. In my mind, selling during this sad period would be a blasphemy to Dad's years of entrepreneurial effort and his hard-earned legacy. Moreover, selling would remove my only familiar haven in the sea of chaos. David disinvested, in late 1981, by returning his stock to our family holding company and accepting a long-term payout.

Elected to the Georgia House of Representatives in 1976, David served six consecutive terms and sat on the Health and Ecology, Special Judiciary, and Banks and Banking Committees. After moving to Atlanta in 1982, he formed D. S. Jerome Productions, Inc., an artistic design firm, and went on to create outstanding photographic art pieces. His "Apres du bord" was the first photograph ever accepted and displayed by the Salon Des Artistes Independants in Paris.

Dolores increased her attacks. She took a shovel and bashed the hood and broke the windshield of my DeLorean. She called the police and lied that I physically assaulted her but had no red marks or bruises to convince the police to arrest me. She threw my silk ties with the swan logo, custom-made shirts, tailored suits and Gucci shoes on the lawn. I grabbed them and stashed them. Finally, in November 1981, I packed up my library, moved out of Brynllawn Road and settled in Norfolk. This ended 16 years of sirloin steaks, baked potatoes and peas but unleashed 10 years of unremitting Lebanese terrorist attacks that made the movement of boundary rocks in the hills of Zahle' seem juvenile.

In late fall 1983, Tres called me and pleaded to live in Norfolk. He had made the same request that summer but, after I had enrolled him in Norfolk Academy, he had changed his mind. This time Tres said he was definitely coming. I flew in my King Air to the Philadelphia airport, picked up Tres at the Shipley School; had him call his Mother to tell her he was leaving with me; and we headed for the airport. Our getaway was a scene from a Laurel and Hardy movie; the getaway car was low on gas so we pulled into a gas station. Just then, two police cars raced by with sirens blaring. Dolores had reported that Tres had been kidnapped. We parked at the edge of the airport until the police left and then boarded our plane for takeoff. After more hearings in the Montgomery County Court, the Judge ruled Tres could live in Norfolk.

While my personal world was being shattered, the international oil world was in turmoil. Iraq invaded Iran on September 22, 1980; crude oil and finished product prices soared. In 1981 President Ronald Reagan abolished United States oil import regulations. Saudi Arabia increased crude oil production and oil prices fell and fell. In those two years, 1980 and 1981, I made 13 international trips for a total of 53 days abroad to negotiate revisions in our contracts with the foreign refineries. Nevertheless, with the remaining fixed-price contracts, the inventory of fuel oils in our terminals and at sea in our tankers, Swann Oil suffered. For the fiscal year ending July 31, 1983, Swann Oil had sales of $400 million, a book loss of $8.8 million and a cash loss, after adding back depreciation, of $5.6 million; and for the five-month period ending December 31, 1983, sales were $162 million, book loss $2 million, and a cash loss, after adding back depreciation, $750,000. They were the first losses in the company's history. This created a technical default in our financing agreement for working capital that supported the $31 million Line of Credit issued by a consortium of banks—American

Bank and Trust Company of Reading, United Virginia Bank of Norfolk, Banque Paribas of Paris and the Bank of Nova Scotia.

With only $14.6 million borrowed from that Line of Credit, I was negotiating with the banks to waive the default until the cash came in from the $5.75 million sale of the oil tanker *Dolores Swann*. With the dramatic decline in ocean freight rates, the *Dolores Swann* had been losing $150,000 per month. Its sale would end a significant cash drain and bring the company to break even for the current fiscal year. I was confident of reaching a revised agreement with the banks, contingent upon the sale of the ship.

At the Philadelphia airport, in early May 1984, after a positive negotiating meeting with the Bank Consortium on the Line of Credit, the Loan Officer of the United Virginia Bank and I were waiting for our commercial flight when suddenly a burly Process Server handed me divorce papers from Dolores. It was the first revelation to the banks that I had any marital difficulties. Their reaction on May 8 was to stand firm on the existing agreement and demand either additional cash investment in the company to cure the cash default or cancellation of the Line of Credit and immediate repayment of the outstanding loan of $14.6 million.

Unknown to the banks, my fallback position was to accept a written offer, received in early May, from BP North American Trading to lease our terminals, tugboats and barges in Pennsylvania and Virginia for 6 years at a minimum net lease of $5.35 million per year. This shift in business strategy would make us landlords in Pennsylvania and Virginia; still leave the three office buildings in Bala Cynwyd for us to rent to third parties; and reduce our direct marketing efforts for petroleum sales and common carrier hauling to Georgia and North Carolina. It would be a profitable but less stressful business enterprise.

On May 23, Dolores filed an emergency petition in Montgomery County Divorce Court alleging that I had hidden $33 million in overseas bank accounts and was selling buildings and the ship to raise more cash in preparation for fleeing the country. Based solely on Dolores' false affidavit, Judge Anthony Scirica froze the company's bank accounts and assets. Not only could no cash be raised from the sale or lease of assets to cure the default, but also no payroll checks could be issued. Swann Oil's only recourse was to file Chapter 11 to have the Federal Bankruptcy Court supersede the Montgomery County Court. On May

25, 1984, Swann Oil, Inc. and its subsidiaries filed for protection under Chapter 11 in the Bankruptcy Court. "The court order won by Mrs. Swann," reported <u>The Philadelphia Inquirer</u> was "the extra nudge that pushed Swann and his oil business into bankruptcy court."

My personal income from the Swann Oil enterprises for the previous two years had been $1.3 million annually but now was reduced by the Trustee to my base salary of $175,000 per year. That salary, after the payment of personal income taxes, was barely enough to cover the Divorce Court's mandated interim monthly support payments to Dolores and the children; the mortgages on the Villanova and Wellfleet houses; and school tuitions. After the Debtor in Possession Exclusivity Period ended on October 1, 1986, I worked with the Trustee as a consultant at $150,000 annual salary to help liquidate assets and reorganize the company but my involvement with Swann Oil and its subsidiaries was very limited. Eventually the Trustee discharged me, thus ending, like a falling guillotine, my consultant paycheck. What an ignoble, embarrassing and impoverishing exit.

Ironically, Dolores would receive nothing from the liquidation of Swann Oil assets. Had she been able to control her Lebanese scorched-earth gene, Swann Oil would have resolved its credit problem; or would have been successfully repositioned by accepting BP North America's lease proposal; or, in the worst scenario, by disposing of the hard assets—trucks, trailers, barges, ship, 9 terminals—plus the liquidation of the inventory and the contract customer base in a fire sale probably would have netted $8 to $10 million after the payment of all debts, which split in a divorce settlement would have been substantial. Moreover, over the course of the next seven years, multiple investigations, depositions, court hearings and extensive audits of both corporate and personal tax returns by independent forensic accountants and the Internal Revenue Service did not discover any missing cash, secret offshore banking accounts, fraudulent transfer of assets, or tax evasion. Not one single penny! I was no Marc Rich breaking the law by trading foreign supplies of oil and hiding scads of cash in multiple foreign accounts. I was a country boy from Sassamansville, who lived his financial life completely above board. There was nothing hidden. In fact, I was so scrupulous that I had filed every Form 942 "Employer's Quarterly Tax Return for Household Employees" for my payments of wages and Social Security for all the household staff and later the daytime attendants for my sick Mother.

Filing Chapter 11 for Swann Oil pushed the panic buttons at United Virginia Bank, which held only 12 percent ($1.75 million) of the outstanding Bank Consortium Line of Credit, but also had $4.2 million of additional loans for my Southern buying spree. First, the former owner of Virginia Materials called the standby Letter of Credit issued by United Virginia Bank for $1.1 million still owed to him on the original purchase price. Since ship traffic had declined in Hampton Roads harbor due to the fall off of exports tied to the value of the United States dollar, Lynnhaven Services was closed down permanently and the marine equipment posted for sale. Cygnet Communications had not turned a profit yet, because it historically required about four years from startup or restructuring for a magazine venture to reach the circulation and advertising revenue necessary to become profitable. The United Virginia Bank forced the consolidation of all debt under the Virginia Materials' umbrella and required my personal guarantee to increase from 50 percent to 100 percent. In essence, the bank took control of everything. Virginia Materials could not carry all the debt, filed Chapter 11 in December 1986, and eventually was liquidated in October 1991.

Depositions of Loan Officers of United Virginia Bank as part of subsequent litigations in Virginia Courts confirmed that it was Dolores' commencement of divorce proceedings and Judge Scirica's order to freeze the Swann Oil accounts that set in motion United Virginia Bank's determined efforts to end its relationship with me. One loan officer testified about the "schizophrenic relationship, where on one hand we are proceeding down an adversary path with Leonard Swann and on the other hand we are continuing to lend . . . he could not honor his personal guarantees." The bank crossed an ethical line when it met with large customers of Virginia Materials—Norshipco and Main Industries—to assess their feelings about my continued ownership of the company. These customers were angry because I had raised the price of Black Blast Abrasive. Subsequently, in the bankruptcy liquidation only three days after closing down the company's operations, a close friend of one of the Bank's Board Members purchased Virginia Materials at a quarter of the depreciated asset value on its balance sheet.

Another Bank Loan Officer added testimony that I was "too global in business planning . . . concern about Dr. Swann's tendency to try to take a business beyond where it might logically go . . . a controversial figure . . . high profile . . . very hard and tough business man . . . difficult to deal with . . . tough negotiator."

"They are going to bankrupt every corporation and upstream and bankrupt me," I testified. "And at the same time it impacted upon the personal divorce litigation because I feared I would lose custody of my son . . . my wife's position was that with the bankruptcy of Swann Oil, I was no longer competent to provide a satisfactory home for my son and that I would have to spend so much time in an attempt to reorganize, I would ignore him. If you overlay the bankruptcy of Virginia Materials, the Cycom Group, and me personally I ran the risk of losing custody of my son. I was under tremendous duress."

With the help of attorney Judith Cofield, a separate suit was filed, under the Racketeer Influenced and Corrupt Organizations Act (RICO), in Federal court against United Virginia Bank and the rest of the Bank Consortium for their interstate conspiracy to control and take over the Swann Oil enterprises and my Virginia companies. I had learned of RICO in 1981, when Frank "The Irishman" Sheeran was convicted in Wilmington, Delaware, for the interstate conspiracy to supply truck drivers under special leases to circumvent paying union wages and benefits. Using the subsequent RICO precedents established by the Mafia Commission and Concrete cases in New York City for expanding the concept of illegal interstate conspiracy was my well-founded counterattack against the banks. But the Judge eventually threw out my civil RICO suit without allowing the trial that I believed would have proved the depth of the banks' conspiracy and the punitive damages owed to our companies and to me.

Whatever the tactics and opinions, I personally owed the United Virginia Bank more than $5 million and my financial life was ended. What had remained after the Swann Oil proceedings, I eventually lost—Virginia Materials, the magazine companies, the Lynnhaven marine equipment, College Place office building, Blanding Street office building, miscellaneous lots in Virginia Beach and Nags Head, my grandparents' farm house near Sassamansville and my cars—a Jaguar, Mercedes and DeLorean.

The indignities had no limits. One Easter morning, as I was preparing to leave for Easter Mass, Lawrence Smith called me. This was the same Lawrence Smith, former President of one of the banks merged into the United Virginia Bank, who attended the Schlesinger Library dinner and flew frequently in our company plane to attend Philadelphia Phillies baseball and Eagles football games in our private stadium box. This was the Lawrence Smith who had enjoyed free office space and all utilities for himself and his staff in my College Place building for more than a year while resurrecting his business life after being summarily terminated in that bank merger. This was the Lawrence Smith who had invited me to invest in Essex Financial, his new company, and also to join him and eight other investors in purchasing two apartment buildings in downtown Norfolk. Lawrence now informed me that all of the partners had voted me out under a special clause in the partnership agreement without a refund of my original investments. To them I was a lunatic, a loser, a leper who had to be exorcised on Easter Sunday.

Nothing was too petty for the leper treatment in Norfolk. I was one of the 42 founders and investors that constituted the permanent Board of Directors of the Town Point Club, a private restaurant and social club at the World Trade Center in Norfolk. Shortly after my Easter phone call, my name was exorcised from the permanent board, which hereafter was published as 41 founders. There would be no "schizophrenic relationship" with a financial leper, nor would there be a refund of my investment.

There was ongoing harassment from Dolores in the Montgomery County Divorce Court, where her actions were designed to delay our divorce. Dolores fought for copies of every check I authorized or signed. She rampaged to deny Tres the right to live with me in Norfolk. I had to appear again and again in Divorce Court. One tactic was to suggest that the time demanded by the bankruptcy proceedings prevented my having any quality time to be a father to Tres. Another tactic was to expose my personal life—"Are you having an intimate relationship with Gayle O'Neal?" The Montgomery Court ordered me to be evaluated by a court-appointed psychiatrist to determine if it were safe for Heather and Tres to be alone with me. "Share with me," the psychiatrist began my session, "everything you remember about your childhood; begin with potty training." I growled, "Yellow from the front and brown from the back" and stormed out, shouting over my shoulder, "You should be examining the crazy one, not me!"

I was called into the Norfolk Court to defend against Dolores' suit that I had enrolled Tres in the inferior Norfolk Academy and therefore he should be returned to her in Villanova so that he could attend a superior prep school on the Main Line. (Founded in 1728, Norfolk Academy was now under the leadership of Headmaster John Tucker, Jr. and was nationally recognized as a leading, independent private school.) Before that hearing, my attorney advised me to volunteer no information but only to answer the Judge's specific questions. "Mr. Swann, do you believe that Norfolk Academy is a good choice as the private school for your son?" . . . "Yes, your Honor." . . ."The Court rules that Tres Swann shall continue to attend Norfolk Academy." When we walked from the court room after this one-minute hearing, my attorney laughed as he informed me that the Judge's wife was Tres' English teacher at Norfolk Academy. Tres continued to live with me.

Balancing my business pressures with my parenting responsibilities— particularly for Tres—was never an "either—or" decision, but always the "and" conjunction. Tres played on the Norfolk Academy Junior Varsity Basketball Team in 1984 and 1985, and I attended all of his games. Tres was interested in deep-sea fishing, and I took him fishing on day charters from Oregon Inlet, North Carolina. We fished regularly from Captain Harry Baum's *Jo Boy II* and Captain Omie Tillet's *The Sportsman*. Fishing presented a relaxed opportunity for Tres to bond with Gayle, who also was enthralled with deep-sea fishing. Her Irish luck frequently prevailed; she usually landed the biggest fish, whether blue marlin, white marlin, sail fish or yellow-fin tuna.

Daughter Heather was particularly upset and refused to have any direct contact with me. Brainwashed by her mother, she felt that I was starving her. "I borrowed $139 for books from my roommate," Heather wrote in September 1984 from Wellesley College. "I have $56, no credit card and no gas card, as you know. Thank you for a life of everything to a life of nothing." Dolores had insisted that Paul Ernest, her minion son, be appointed trustee of both of Heather's trusts, which the court approved. Nevertheless, I was mystified because Heather's 1975 trust had ample cash to cover her college tuition and expenses. And there appeared to be substantial earnings from her Ashley Meadows Farm 1979 trust. What was happening to the money when

Heather, the sole beneficiary, was receiving nothing for college? Plus Heather was occasionally leaving Wellesley on weekends to compete in horse shows. What was the source of that money? Nevertheless, I paid all of Heather's college expenses at Wellesley. I was not invited to her graduation. After graduating from Wellesley, Heather entered the University of Pennsylvania School of Veterinary Medicine in September 1989.

My other daughters called with the occasional emergency. Debby, after graduating from Philadelphia College of Art, became a hippie artist and wandered for several years through Europe and California. In early 1980, she called in desperation from California where she was stranded and broke. After I wired her money to return to Philadelphia, she announced that she wanted to study law at Cardozo School of Law at Yeshiva University in New York City. "You have to be kidding me," was my reaction. "I don't know which is worse, a hippy artist or a lawyer? I'll pay for law school and living expenses in New York only if you carry a full course load and maintain a minimum B average." Debby maintained that average, secured a student fellowship to work with U.S. District Judge Harold Ackerman, received her law degree in 1985, passed her bar exam, and landed a position at the Tax Division of the Department of Justice.

Rachael graduated from the University of Pennsylvania, married Edward Vitale and moved to New Brunswick, New Jersey, for graduate studies in Biology at Rutgers, the State University of New Jersey. At the end of her last semester, she called with a major problem. Ed was a General Contractor in a partnership that remodeled houses. Their partnership had purchased a two-apartment building, where both partners were living. Ed wanted to sell his share, the downstairs apartment, to relocate with Rachael when she began her studies at the University of Pennsylvania School of Veterinary Medicine. Ed's partner refused to buy out Ed's share or to sell the entire property. It was the classic stalemate. I went to meet the partner. "I've just entered a long-term lease with Ed Vitale, my son-in-law, for the downstairs apartment," I told him. "I'm a zealous Catholic and have been asked by Sister Edmundine of the Bernadine Convent to help with their mission of providing temporary housing for unwed, pregnant, homeless girls. I plan to donate this apartment to the Bernadine Sisters for their mission. I just wanted you to know so that you won't be surprised by the parade of new tenants." One week later, Ed had a contract for the sale of his share of the building at a fair price to his ex-partner. Rachael was on her way to Veterinary School and graduated in 1985.

In late 1986, Rachael asked for help in buying a farm in Keysville, Virginia, to build a rural veterinary clinic. She had surveyed rural areas in different states and finally had selected Keysville as the idealistic haven from the crassness of metropolitan living. With my Sassamansville heritage, I could understand her decision. I gave her a gift for the down payment, and she opened Simplicity Animal Hospital. Then, Rachael assessed the local schools and decided to home school her two sons, Morgan and Matthew. "Your plan for home schooling is not fair to Morgan," "I wrote. "It is easy for common sense to be overshadowed by myopic concentration on the pursuit of an idealized life-style. Perhaps a similar quest was best charted in the book <u>Mosquito Coast</u>, where the obsessive father retreats from the modern world to recreate a civilization in the wilderness had disastrous effects on the family and children." I included a copy of the book <u>Mosquito Coast</u>. Rachael ignored my letter and the book, went forward with her plan to home school at the same time that she was running her veterinary clinic, later watched the movie <u>Mosquito Coast</u>, continued to home school all her children, and didn't discuss education with me again during any of our infrequent contacts.

A surprise letter with a Saint Croix postmark arrived from Judy's son, Paul Alexander, in the summer of 1981. It was the first contact I ever had with him. I had paid child support while his mother was flitting from marriage to marriage and living for years in Saint Croix in the Caribbean. Paul asked me to pay his tuition and board at Lehigh University in Bethlehem, which I agreed to do. Then in 1983, he requested a meeting in person to discuss his moving from the dormitory to an apartment. I met him at Lehigh for my first and only sight of him. I decided he had his mother's grifter gene, turned down the apartment request—"Cherchez la femme"—and never saw him again. However, I did pay his tuition and dormitory expenses for all four years at Lehigh.

Gayle had always dreamed of owning either an upscale coffee house or a collectable doll store. In early 1983, she opened My Doll House at Waterside, Norfolk's new waterfront center designed to duplicate Baltimore's successful Inner Harbor. She included a

Gone-With-The-Wind museum display to attract the tourists. In 1984, she opened a second store in Williamsburg, near Busch Gardens; and in 1986 a third store, also with a Gone-With-The-Wind museum display, at the upscale La Promanade Shopping Center in Virginia Beach. The Virginia Beach location soon had more sales than the Norfolk and Williamsburg stores combined. Gayle closed those two stores in 1988, but added regional weekend doll shows to her marketing efforts. Her children, Jackie, Jennifer and Ari, worked at the store through high school and college. I helped on weekends and viewed the doll shows as our mini-adventures together.

Gayle had an instinct for the doll collectors' tastes; the ability to walk the aisles at the annual New York Toy Fair and the Atlanta Gift Show and recognize hot new items; and a flair for retail display and customer schmoozing. One year at the New York Toy Fair, she placed a large order for Madame Alexander's Scarlett Jubilee II Series to commemorate the 50th anniversary of the movie <u>Gone With The Wind</u>. The series included dolls depicting Scarlett, Rhett, Melanie, Ashley and Mammy. Gayle also had designed an exclusive, limited edition 10-inch Southern Belle doll, which the Alexander Doll Company manufactured for her. She carried her first incoming shipment of these very collectable dolls to a doll show in Atlanta and sold $22,000 worth of dolls in eight hours! Watching Gayle develop her dream ranked high in the few positive moments during this period of my life.

To the rest of the world, I was just an embarrassing outcast from Pennsylvania and a shunned renegade in Virginia. I had to file Chapter 7 in Bankruptcy Court in early 1991 in order to cut off all personal liabilities, particularly from the machinations of the United Virginia Bank; the only possessions the Court permitted me to keep were my clothes, books and ownership in the joint, personal residences. I was the first Swann to file for personal bankruptcy. Uncle Vernon's voice kept haunting me with "Smart muckers do not finish at the tail end!"

On November 30, 1991, almost 10 years to the day after my separation, my divorce from the paranoid, punitive and pompous Dolores was entered. She received sole titles to the Villanova and Wellfleet houses—with a combined value of $2 million and a mortgage on Villanova of less than $90,000—and alimony of $4,000 a month for 48 months. She had succeeded in her Lebanese Torquemada vengeance by undermining my reputation in the petroleum, publishing and financial worlds, mutilating my corporate finances, exacerbating my hemorrhaging $30 million in personal net worth, thus completely ruining me and leaving me with nothing. Dolores had her schadenfreude and I had obliteration; however, I thought of Vince Lombardi, the legendary coach of the Green Bay Packers, and his observation—"It's not whether you get knocked down, it's whether you get up." My getting up was very questionable.

As I stressed over the disintegration of my economic life and the decade of incessant Lebanese divorce tactics, I was especially saddened by how lonely and isolated my life had become. From the hundreds and hundreds of business associates listed in my personal rolodex, dozens of personal and corporate attorneys, more than 700 employees in multiple companies—with 25 in top management who worked very closely with me—and scores and scores of relatives, I discovered that I was surrounded by strangers who I thought were my friends. Only 14 people stood beside me, facing into the wind. Only 14 people stood by me, expressed any concern about me and made me feel less alone.

Heading the Band of Fourteen was Gayle. Despite a decade of withering attacks in court proceedings, intrusive surveillance by private investigators and Dolores' harassing phone calls, Gayle held my hand, loved me unconditionally and made me feel whole and complete. She validated my existence, through richer and poorer, when others questioned and disparaged it. And she had that infectious smile that lit up any gloomy room.

My Mother protected me as only a mother can. I limped away with only my clothes and books but found refuge with Mother, who had moved to Norfolk to live with me. "Come in she said," in the words of Bob Dylan, "I'll give you shelter from the storm." I was grateful and humble that Mother wanted to spend her remaining years with me. Once while doing dishes together, I joked Mother that I now knew more Latin then I had known in high school, when she had grounded me with dish duty. I spouted "Illegitimi non carborundum," which I translated very loosely as "never let the bastards get you down," Dad's mantra, which was so very appropriate now.

My son Tres, at the age of 14, made the decision to live with me. He endured multiple court appearances, withstood a barrage of threats and resisted his mother's attempted bribe of a large motorboat in Wellfleet for his return to living with her. (As his mother wrote to Tres, "The boat

is 'all set' . . . it will be waiting to 'Amuse you' upon your return.")
Tres chose to stay at my side. His academic achievements at Norfolk
Academy and the College of William and Mary made me proud.

My brother David stayed in contact from Atlanta, commiserated
about failed marriages and offered to give me the last $11,000 from his
savings account if I needed it for living expenses.

Uncle Joe constantly encouraged me to "hang in there," and
reminded me of Grandma's "There is always a better tomorrow." He
made trips from Sassamansville to Norfolk to check that our family
at Bull Run Court was hanging in there and even attended a surprise
40th birthday party for Gayle. Until his death in March 1988, Uncle
Joe was my active link to both Dad and Father Letterhouse. Plus he
shared his short memoir jottings on Swann family traditions and his
country poems to boost my resolve and spirits—for example, "Things
That Count" —

> Life's good important things are the simple things I've found.
> A little ray of sunshine;
> A penny on the ground;
> A true friend, and a kindness;
> A life that's free from sin;
> A little smile from those you love;
> And a little nip of gin.

Janet Smith, my administrative assistant in Pennsylvania; Bill
Berkey, the company's first oil burner serviceman; Ralph Bass,
superintendent of the Chesapeake Terminal and Virginia Materials;
and Hank Blessing, a truck mechanic from Sassamansville who had
relocated to the Chesapeake Terminal—these four were the only former
employees who maintained any contact and offered to help me!

Frank Freidel called occasionally from Harvard to check on me, to
encourage my resuming research for the history of the Brooklyn Naval
Yard and to return to teaching.

Brian Graves, my former British broker for marine insurance at
Lloyd's of London, maintained contact with letters and visits. When he
traveled to the United States, Brian would include Bull Run Court in his
itinerary, stay overnight at our house and continue our ongoing debate
about Admiral Horatio Nelson's tactics at the Battle of the Nile and

Trafalgar. Gayle and I had a standing invitation to vacation at Brian's house in West Sussex, England.

Frank Dunn, Gayle's older brother, always sensed the right moment to take me to lunch for a pep talk similar to Dad's "never let the bastards get you down."

And attorneys Alan Boroff for divorce representation and Frank Santoro for bankruptcy representation were dedicated advocates and sincere advisers for years, even though they knew that I could not pay all of their out-of-pocket expenses and legal fees. I was forever indebted to them.

To this list must be added one more—Shadow's Sassylass of Scotchhill, better known as Sassy, my Burmese cat. When Tres moved to Norfolk, he missed his pet cat in Villanova. Sassy, a kitten, was purchased as a replacement. But Sassy did not bond with Tres. This beautiful Burmese, with her soft brown coat and expressive gold eyes, chose me. How ironic, since I was totally indifferent to pets. For the next decade, Sassy became my shadow. She sat in the window when I left in the morning. She ran down the hall to meet me when I entered the front door. She purred on my lap as I read in my study. She guarded my bed as I slept. Every day began with a "Good Morning, Sassy" and her responding purr. And her name was my daily reminder of my roots.

Once again, William Shakespeare authored a sage summary of my predicament. "Who steals my purse steals trash," Shakespeare's Iago said in Othello. "But he that filches from me my good name . . . makes me poor indeed." And Cassio added: "Reputation, reputation, reputation! O, I have lost my reputation, I have lost the immortal part of myself." I ended this period of my life with neither purse, nor reputation.

Hustle Days

There I was, in the early 1990's, a black swan, staring at a lake of desolation, occasionally flapping my wings but not really flying, breathing but not really living; a beached, busted and boring black swan. I was 52 years old and living with my Mother. I was educated but had no economic life, no exciting occupation or predictable income. I was self-disciplined and did not smoke or consume drugs, alcohol, caffeine or red meat but so what. I was a black swan starting "the only true voyage of discovery," which as Marcel Proust wrote, "is not to go to new places but to have other eyes."

But my eyes were full of floaters—the floaters of defeat, desertion, deflation, destitution, despair and depression. These floaters kept reminding me where I'd been and they were coagulating to dictate where I was going. These floaters were momentary distractions from my Sassamansville determination for survival.

One day I bumped into Colonel Carl Moulton, a good old boy from the Virginia hills. He was an auctioneer; good auctioneers in the South were often called "Colonel" and were usually scavenging for one person's detritus to turn into another person's treasure at the next auction. "Sorry to hear about your bad luck," Colonel Moulton volunteered. "But I'll tell you what—what you need is a hustle. Think hustle, hustle, hustle. Get you a pickup and become 'Chuck with a truck' and hustle."

Where had I heard and experienced the word "hustle" before? Dad had his hustles—dump truck, coal truck, oil truck, service truck, mail truck, tractor-trailer truck, tires for trucks, and even truck-driving music from his country western band. My hustles had included oil ships, tug boats, barges, launches, railcars, oil terminals, manufacturing plants and magazines. Colonel Moulton triggered my epiphany. I had the hustle gene. I had to hustle but forget about the pickup truck. I already had the vehicle for my rejuvenating and survival hustles—Specialty Products.

In 1988, while Tres was a student at Norfolk Academy, Specialty Products, Inc. had been formed. Tres, at age 18, had complete ownership and was President. My original purpose was to have a nascent entity to teach Tres the fundamentals of business—like my Dad had taught me—and to have the generation of profits excite him and distract him from the pitfalls of the average teenager. Tres played drums, had formed a rock band with three buddies from Norfolk Academy and practiced after school at our home on Bull Run Court. He began dabbling with a four-track recording system. I envisioned Tres going astray in the Rock Band Culture. But I hoped that Specialty Products would stimulate his business gene. (One of the school parents had asked how I could stand teenage boys and their band noise in our house. "It's simple," I replied. "I can relax since I know firsthand that they are a nice group of boys; what they are doing is a wholesome activity; my Mother is in the house to keep a protective eye on them; moreover, I'm not ferrying Tres and his drums back and forth to someone else's house." It made perfect sense to me.)

Specialty Products won a bid contract to supply safety gloves to the Portsmouth Naval Shipyard. The gloves were purchased wholesale, relabeled by Tres and delivered to the shipyard. Specialty Products made its first profit. More miscellaneous small government orders for blast nozzles and containment tarps followed. While Tres was studying at William and Mary College, I turned to Specialty Products as the entity to rebuild my business life.

During its Chapter 11 existence, the Trustee of Virginia Materials would not commit funds for the normal maintenance of the plant's equipment. The tractor-trucks began to break down. Surprisingly, the Trustee accepted a proposal to lease tractors and other small equipment, on a month-by-month basis, from Specialty Products. Eight pieces of used equipment, tractors and bulk trailers, were purchased by Specialty Products and leased to Virginia Materials. Also, a 32-ton steel storage hopper, air compressors and forklifts were leased. These rentals produced a steady, profitable revenue stream until Virginia Materials was shut down temporarily in October 1991 for a liquidation sale to a new owner.

The market niche that Virginia Materials filled was surface preparation. My brief experience there made my hustle radar sensitive to any competitive product or technology that addressed surface preparation. The first to cross my radar was DuPont Starblast from DuPont Titanium Technologies.

At its Florida plant, DuPont produced Starblast, a unique mineral abrasive as a byproduct from separating titanium dioxide from the mined ore. Compared to Virginia Materials' Black Blast from coal slag, Starblast was 30 percent more efficient, less dusty and environmentally better because it contained virtually no carcinogenic materials, such as silicon dioxide, arsenic, lead and cadmium. I secured a Starblast distributorship for Specialty Products and now had a superior blasting abrasive to compete with Black Blast. Orders grew from regular accounts—for instance, the shipyards and the Virginia electric power plants—for bulk trailer loads direct from DuPont's Florida plant; and for the year 1990, DuPont honored Specialty Products with the DuPont "Partners in Progress" award for outstanding Starblast sales.

Coincidentally, Wheelabrator Corporation introduced the Blastrac, a portable, self-contained, recycling blasting machine that was ideal for cleaning and profiling concrete floors or steel ship decks in preparation for the application of coatings. Wheelabrator had developed the technology for its large stationary machinery that was used in the steel mills to clean millscale and rust from steel plates. This revolutionary portable Blastrac was replacing open-air nozzle blasting. We rushed to secure a distributorship for this Blastrac equipment.

Selling Blastrac was just another hustle like my teenage days of selling oil burner service, fuel oil tanks and car tires. The customer needed a Blastrac to profile either concrete floors to create a bond for enamel paint, or steel ship decks for painting or installing non-skid coatings. Initially, the customer rented a Blastrac unit from our rental fleet, which was financed for distributors by the manufacturer's rent-to-own program. When the customer had confidence in the Blastrac and a backlog of work, he would usually purchase a machine. Specialty Products backed up the equipment with skilled service mechanics and in-house parts inventory. Fred Clarke was hired as Sales Manager, and Gail Zeitlin as Comptroller. With the encouragement of William Marsh and Wayne Benitz at Blastrac, Specialty Products generated sales along the East Coast and even in South America, where my old contacts were helpful. For eight consecutive years, 1990 through 1997, Specialty Products had the highest sales of any Blastrac distributor in the United States and won the annual plaque and bonus from the manufacturer, including cruises to the Caribbean.

When United Virginia Bank foreclosed on the College Place office, I scurried to rent 1200 square feet of office space in a new building at 5660 East Virginia Beach Boulevard in Norfolk. The owner also had an adjacent industrial building, where he manufactured kitchen cabinets. About six months later, depressed by financial pressures and a pending divorce, he parked his car inside his cabinet plant, kept the engine running and committed suicide by carbon monoxide poisoning. A week after his death, his widow had an auctioneer advertising the sale of his cabinet-making equipment; and she had her attorney contact me, the only tenant, about purchasing the two buildings for a minimum cash payment to her and the assumption of the existing mortgage. I set up 5660 Realty Company for Tres with financing from his 1975 Trust for the widow's payment to seal the purchase of this property. Tres, at age 20, had a prime piece of real estate.

One night in summer 1990, Gayle and I decided on a whim to have dinner at the Upper Deck in Virginia Beach and catch Bill Deal and the Rhondels with Fat Ammons on the drums. Bill Deal was a local celebrity made famous by his recordings "May I" and "What Kind of Fool Do You Think I Am," which had been high on the national charts in the late Sixties. The TFC Band was the warm-up act and replicated the sound of The Drifters with cover songs from the Fifties and Sixties—"Sugar Pie Honey" . . ."Ain't that Peculiar" . . ."Magic Moment" . . ."Same Old Song" . . ."Sixty Minute Man" . . ."Wooly Bully," and my favorite, "Under the Boardwalk." The TFC Band was talented and very entertaining.

In November 1990, I hired the TFC Band to play at Gayle's Daughter Jennifer's wedding reception at the Cavalier Hotel. In fall 1991, we were returning late from a doll show and stopped at the Show Place, a restaurant-nightclub on the Eastern Shore for a quick dinner, where coincidentally the TFC Band was performing. There were about a dozen people in the audience. During the break, I asked the front men what they were doing in this small venue. They replied that they had difficulty securing bookings. With impulsive bravado, I offered to be their exclusive manager and agent for booking all gigs for 20 percent commission off the top. They agreed. Sirocco Productions, Inc. was set up, with Gayle as the owner, to be the official booking agency; and the TFC Band signed an exclusive contract in October 1991. The choice of the name "Sirocco" was my private joke. A sirocco is a hot, dusty wind from a desert; and I was initially blowing hot air when I became a booking agent. After all, Grandma Swann always said, "You can do anything you want to do."

Having watched Dick Clark's "American Bandstand" in her teenage days, Gayle suggested what the TFC Band needed was a promotional video of its talented act. Having watched Bob Horn's "Bandstand," Dick Clark's predecessor, I agreed. Sirocco rented the video studio at Creative Edge in Chesapeake. Gayle and I directed the video shoot and editing of a 15-minute promotional video, <u>The TFC Band, Music of the Fifties and Sixties</u>.

I started hustling engagements for the TFC Band. Over the next 34 months, I secured venues in eight states and Canada, booked 356 playing days, and earned $45,000 of commissions for Sirocco. But managing the TFC Band was one minor disaster after another. Their van and tow trailer broke down on the way to Texas, and the band missed a big engagement there. On another trip, their electric keyboard and sound system were stolen and had to be replaced. During a month of scheduled performances in California, the band members enjoyed California so much that they spent their entire gross income and needed money wired for expenses to return home. A wife of one of the front men decided that she could manage the band better and could find enough local engagements to avoid the long-distance traveling. So in mid-1994, the TFC Band reneged on its contract and ended Sirocco's exclusivity. This part-time hustle was fun but proved that I did not have Uncle Russell's patience or night owl personality to schmooze in show business and that I would not be reincarnated as an entertainment mogul.

While working a weekend doll show, in late 1991, at Gaithersburg, Maryland, with Gayle, I was fascinated by the importance of dolls, which originated as playthings contributing to a child's emotional and social growth, but also were an art form and objective correlative that conveyed historical, cultural and social meaning. Many doll enthusiasts seemed to make their purchases on emotion or whim but lacked accurate information on what they were collecting and often had no appreciation or understanding of a doll's broader meaning. For instance, the average doll collector could identify the Gone-With-The-Wind characters but many were confused by the various editions, costumes and market value of Scarlett dolls created by Madame Alexander and other designers; and few had a grasp of the significant historical context.

Fresh from our video experience with the TFC Band video, Gayle and I sat there brainstorming the possibilities of creating a documentary video on Scarlett dolls. Gayle had contacts in the doll world for borrowing the historical Scarlett dolls. She had the flair for display needed for set design and skill in tweaking miniature costumes. I had the background in research, writing and storytelling. We both had the "eye" for framing the camera shots and editing the cuts to assemble a visual story. And we both had the "hustle."

Call it "fate" or "dumb luck" but the next morning I was early for an appointment with my optometrist. His wife and receptionist, Jan Lebow, engaged in idle chatter and inquired about what was keeping me busy. "Oh, Gayle and I have started a video production company," I boasted. "We've been thinking about producing a documentary video on Scarlett O'Hara dolls." Her face lit up. "Did you know that I have collected Scarlett dolls for years?" she asked. "I'm writing a book entitled The Fashion History of Alexander Scarlett O'Hara Dolls. Perhaps you would like to video my collection, for credit of course, for your documentary." My eyeballs almost popped out in disbelief—almost creating more business for her husband—as I accepted her offer.

The video was shot at Creative Edge. Gayle and I researched and wrote the script and were co-producers. We borrowed original photos and artifacts form Herb Bridges, an author and authority on both the book and movie version of Gone With The Wind. Jan Lebow and Gayle set up the scenes for 85 different dolls. Scarlett Dolls, An Alexander Tradition, 1937-1991 was released in late 1991 as the first video in the Sirocco Historical Doll Series. This 72-minute program was an encyclopedic presentation of the evolution of Madame Alexander's Scarlett O'Hara dolls from initial composition models through hard plastic, vinyl and porcelain, and included Gone-With-The-Wind memorabilia and rare photographs of Madame Alexander with her Scarlett dolls. This production also introduced us to Duncan Brown, a videographer and editor, and Lee Lively, a narrator for the voice-over; both would continue as key members of our production team.

Reception of the <u>Scarlett Dolls</u> video among doll collectors was favorable. Moreover, Patricia Burns and Marsha Hunter, nationally recognized experts on Alexander dolls, suggested the need for a documentary on the Dionne Quintuplets, the famous Canadian sisters born in 1934, and Madame Alexander, the inventive New York doll maker, who had the exclusive license and rights to produce Dionne Quintuplet dolls. The reported authorities on the Quintuplets and Quintuplet collectibles were James and Faye Radolfos, respectively a quadriplegic and paraplegic, living in Worcester, Massachusetts. They had turned their house into a private Quintuplet museum. The Radolfos agreed that Sirocco could access their collection, with one practical provision: the videography had to occur in their house and in their presence. Sirocco purchased a video camera, monitors and portable lighting system. Gayle, Walt Altice as videographer, my brother David as photographer for still pictures and slides, and I travelled to Worcester for two weeks of immersion in the Dionne Quintuplets.

The resulting documentary, <u>Dionne Quintuplet Dolls, An Alexander Exclusive, 1934-1939</u>, was 84-minutes long, released in fall 1992, and the second in the Sirocco Historical Doll Series. The video covered the first five years of the five famous sisters and presented the 41 different composition and rag doll sets—of course, five dolls to a set—with movie-news clips, rare contemporary photographs, newspaper advertising featuring the Quints, memorabilia and toy accessories. The "Quintuplets Lullaby" was recorded for the background music.

The <u>Dionne Quintuplet Dolls</u> established Sirocco's reputation. "From first tight close-up of a doll's features," wrote Marceil Drake, an authority on the Quints, "I was in 'teary-land'! From then on it was uphill! I heard things about the Quints and dolls I had never heard before."

"I thought the Dionne presentation even better than that on the Scarlett dolls," wrote Professor Frank Freidel from Harvard. "Not only does it present the dolls in a way that should bring you the collectors' market, but with the research you have done on the Quints, you have turned out a first rate piece of social history. I remember the frenzy of excitement over the Quints . . . but much of what you presented was new to me. You should be in the same business as Ken Burns and David McCullough."

During the shooting of the Dionne video, I heard a rumor that the Colemans were interested in making a video on antique dolls. The Colemans—the mother Dorothy and her daughters, Elizabeth Ann and Evelyn Jane—were recognized world-wide as the authorities on antique dolls from their books—The Collector's Encyclopedia of Dolls and The Collector's Book of Dolls' Clothes. In summer 1992, I met with Dorothy and Jane in their Washington, D.C. home. "Mr. Swann," Dorothy began as she pointed to three antique dolls on the fireplace mantle, "which Jumeau do you like best?" With a déjà vu panic of failing my oral exam at Harvard for an "I don't know," I answered, "Mrs. Coleman, I don't know. That's why I came to you because I want to be educated by the world's expert." She smiled. We reached a royalty agreement; the Coleman's supplied the research, preliminary script and primary collection of French, German and American dolls for Sirocco's production of Dolls of the Golden Age, 1880-1915. It was released in 1993 and received a Four Star rating. The first run of 500 VHS copies sold out immediately, plus the video had to be duplicated in PAL format for sales in England and Germany and SECAM format for sales in France.

Also in production was The Coronation Story for release in 1993, the 40th Anniversary of the Coronation of Queen Elizabeth II. This documentary traced Princess Elizabeth dolls from the 1930's and forty years of Queen Elizabeth dolls. It featured the special tableau of one-of-a-kind, elaborately costumed dolls portraying the Coronation Ceremonies, created by Madame Alexander for display at the Abraham and Straus Department Store in 1953 and then displayed in the permanent collection at the Brooklyn Children's Museum. With the Coleman's recommendation, the Brooklyn Children's Museum sent the collection of 36 dolls to our video studio in Norfolk. It was the first time this tableau would be available on video.

When Tres graduated from William and Mary College in 1992, he could return to a small distribution business chugging along with DuPont and Blastrac products and a video production company taking off for a niche audience. Instead, Tres planned to attend Graduate School. Later that summer, Tres announced that he liked the thought of growing Specialty Products with me and also wanted to start his own record label and recording studio. I was both flabbergasted and excited with the prospect of interacting with Tres on a daily basis in business like my Dad did with me. It was a dream come true.

Tres organized Trumpeter Records, Pen/Cob Publishing and Cygnet Studios with a 24-track digital and analog recording and editing suites in a sound-proof wing of our warehouse. His first release, in October 1992, was "One Good Eye" by the Norfolk band, On Beyond Zee. Other releases followed, among them—"Bonefinger" by Sea of Souls; "Drowning in the Promised Land" by Egypt; "Vice Verses" by Psycho Johnny; "Color of the Day" by the Mundahs; and "Everything" by Everything. Tres had the Dave Matthews Band scheduled to record its first album but two days before the start, Dave Matthews received an offer from a national label and asked Tres to release him, which Tres did.

Tres' building the sound studio was beneficial to Sirocco. Now there was studio space that could be used for the video shoots, since we already owned the camera, monitors and lighting systems. The sound booths were available for the voice-overs and the entire music studio and editing suite for creating the background sound tracks. Later, we would add a video editing suite to become a totally self-sufficient production company.

Opportunities for Sirocco were limited only by our time and resources to develop them. From Naperville, Illinois, Marge Meisinger, an authority on Shirley Temple dolls and collectibles, volunteered her expertise and extensive collection to help produce a video history. The Shirley Temple doll, first released by Ideal Novelty and Toy Company in 1934, became the greatest selling character doll in history. Shirley Temple Dolls & Memorabilia, produced by Sirocco, 90 minutes long, covered 60 years of composition, vinyl and porcelain dolls and other Shirley Temple collectibles. It was released in 1994.

Also in production for Wheelabrator were product videos, averaging 15 minutes in length, on the various models of Blastrac equipment working at industrial sites; a few of these product videos were released in Spanish language versions. Sirocco produced 28-minute infomercials for local television to market My Doll House's exclusive collectibles—the Southern Bell, the Elizabeth I and Empress Elizabeth of Austria dolls made by Alexander Doll Company; the Elizabeth Coronation Bear by Canterbury Bears in England; the Southern Bear by Steiff in Germany; and the Belle du Sud doll by Corolle in France.

But the biggest surprise of all was securing an exclusive license from the Strong Museum in Rochester, New York, for access to its world-renown doll and toy collection for the production of history videos. Under the supervision of Ellen Manyon, the Curator of the Doll Collection, The Doll Makers, Women Entrepreneurs, 1865-1945 was released in 1995. This documentary, 90 minutes in length, portrayed the American women entrepreneurs who made play dolls that were huggable, safe and culturally seminal. It featured Charity Smith, Julia Beecher, Rose O'Neill, Grace Storey Putman, Madame Alexander, Dewees Cochran and many others. The historical significance of doll making was that it was one of the few professions, besides nursing and teaching, that women had access to and actually dominated.

Also, during our multiple video shoots at the Strong Museum, Sirocco recorded a source library for future programs on French and German doll makers and a history of Marx toys. Most important were the enthusiastic recommendations from the Strong Museum to other serious collectors to encourage their support of Sirocco projects. Rollie Adams, the Director of the Strong Museum, paved the way for the Raggedy Ann video with Patricia Hall, the authority on Johnny Gruelle and Raggedy Ann, and Kim Gruelle, the grandson of Johnny Gruelle. Released in 1995, Raggedy Ann & Andy: Johnny Gruelle's Dolls with Heart became the fastest seller of our videos.

"I was initially hesitant about the project," I told a reporter for Dolls magazine in February 1996. "If you've seen one Raggedy Ann you've seen them all . . . red is such a difficult color to deal with on video . . . when you do these videos, you have all sorts of problems: egos, tension while filming, finding the right sets and costumes. Yet on the Raggedy Ann set, we encountered none of these problems . . . It must be the magic of these dolls which are so innately good."

The list of Sirocco videos continued with Doll Art, featuring modern doll artists at the Santa Fe Doll Art Convention in 1996; Les Petites Dames de Mode, a history of Victorian and Edwardian fashions on costumed mannequins by John Burbidge; and Oz: The American Fairyland, 115-minutes long, with the help of Janet Anderson, Michael Hearn, Jay Scarfone and William Stillman, renowned authorities and collectors of dolls and ephemera from The Wonderful World of Oz and L. Frank Baum. "There have been several earlier television documentaries about Oz and Baum, but none has had the scope or depth of Swann's work," wrote Stephen Teller, Professor of English at Pittsburgh (Kansas) State University, in his review of <u>Oz: The American Fairyland</u>. "No presentation of Oz is omitted . . . one aspect of the video that was particularly satisfying was the background score . . . from Jack Graves for the unmade animation film of <u>The Wonderful Wizard of Oz</u>, played by the Seattle Philharmonic Orchestra."

Sirocco produced <u>Cissy, An Alexander Fashion Legend</u>, using the superb collection of Joseph Carrillo; video biographies or artist vignettes, released under the Sirocco Master Artist Series, of Madame Alexander, Helen Bullard, Dewees Cochran, Jane Coleman, Suzanne Gibson, Charles Santore, Catherine Refabert, Robin Woods, Paul Crees and Peter Coe, Judy Brown and Wendy Lawton; convention program videos for the 50th anniversary of the United Federation of Doll Clubs and for five Madame Alexander Doll Club national events; and <u>The Valentine & Expressions of Love</u> with Nancy Rosen's script and remarkable collection of antique valentines, which traced the evolution of this premier love token in the English-speaking world.

Virginia Ann Heyerdahl approached Sirocco to consider Hitty dolls for a documentary video. Virginia Ann Heyerdahl was the authority on Rachael Field and her 6-1/4-inch, hand-carved wooden-doll, whose travels in <u>Hitty: Her First Hundred Years</u>, published in 1929, ranked slightly behind Tom Sawyer in American literature. It won the John Newberry Medal from the American Library Association for the most distinguished child's book of 1929. Rachael Field was the first woman so honored.

Virginia invited me to survey a collection of Hitty dolls during the 1998 New York Toy Fair. Arriving at Virginia's hotel suite about 8 PM, I was totally surprised to walk into a Hitty pajama party. There were about 40 female Hittites, dressed in pajamas and nightgowns, each carrying her favorite Hitty doll in one hand and a cocktail in the other. I was the only male in the room. For a nanosecond, I was really liking Hitty but I retreated from that pajama party faster than I had exited Judy-Ludy's living room during high school.

Very persistent, Virginia sent me a paperback copy of <u>Hitty: Her First Hundred Years</u>, which I threw in my beach bag. A month later, bored at the beach, I read it. I was hooked from Hitty's opening monologue: "The first words I ever heard," said Hitty, "were Phoebe's . . . 'the doll has a face . . . nothing is ever going to happen to her . . . because she will always be my doll.'" As I sat on the beach, I outlined the video program in the margins of the Hitty paperback.

Sirocco released <u>Hitty: An American Travel Doll</u> in late 1998. It featured rare photographs and our video footage of the original Hitty doll in the Library at Stockbridge, Massachusetts. Virginia Ann Heyerdahl and Sirocco cosponsored three national Friends of Hitty Conventions in Williamsburg, including a "Red Hat" Hitty banquet (but this time the Hittites were fully dressed). Sirocco also produced <u>Hitty: The Legend Continues</u> and <u>Hitty, A Carver's Classic</u>. "One of the best the company has produced," was the review in <u>Doll News</u>. Sirocco designed and manufactured three special Hitty dolls, all hand carved and hand painted; plus a Crees-Coe limited-edition porcelain Isabella Van Rensselaer doll, wearing her "Meeting Charles Dickens" costume and holding a three-inch wooden Hitty, hand carved by Judy Brown.

The characteristics and demographics of the doll collector community—both the serious collector and the hobbyist—were very eclectic. The serious collector—those for example, specializing in French and German antique dolls of the 1880's to 1910's or specific themes like Scarlett O'Hara, the Dionne Quintuplets, Shirley Temple, the Wizard of Oz and Hitty—were cultural and social historians. They started with a specific book, theme or doll and researched the author, artist and designer; the manufacturer; the technology employed; the distribution; and the targeted audience from which they assembled a composite picture of the cultural impact. The hobbyist began with a visceral interest—I like Shirley Temple—and purchased the doll to satisfy a craving, to relive happy memories from their youth or simply to possess and enjoy the doll.

The demographics of the serious collector, the supporting doll artists and the doll dealers covered an interesting spectrum. There were many school teachers, both female and male. There were professional fashion designers, whose primary occupation centered on designing popular women's clothing and costumes for Broadway theatre productions. There were women entrepreneurs, whose entire business identity came from writing articles and books on dolls, running doll boutiques or selling at weekend doll shows. There were flea-market dealers who owned big Recreational Vehicles (RV's) and traveled from doll show to doll show, with their hustle of buying and selling, but always looking for the undervalued doll in one regional show that might be in hot demand in another region. Interestingly, a few of the flea-marketers with their RV's reminded me of Uncle Jim and Aunt Lou, hustling and traveling their carnival life.

Husbands of doll collectors or doll dealers, whom I met, represented a variety of occupations. One doll carver's husband worked for the government—wink . . . wink—which translated meant that he was an analyst in the Central Intelligence Agency. Other occupations disclosed were a Commander in the Coast Guard; a Politician on the County Zoning Board; a Purchasing Agent at a military base; a staff member of the General Services Administration; a family doctor; a cosmetic surgeon; a barber; a vendor who drove a van to resupply candy and potato chips to his own vending machines; and a plumber, who gave me leads on flooring work at Quantico, the Marine Corps base in Northern Virginia. I kept quiet about my background and was known primarily as a producer of collector videos with a side business of selling equipment for surface preparation.

At one Hitty Convention, I met Bill Jackson, the husband of a Hitty collector. As we chatted, Bill revealed that he was a sourcing engineer for a company that was refurbishing surplus Canadian military helicopters for sale to the Israeli Army. He was frustrated in his search for special material needed to repair the fiberglass fuselage. My hustle ears perked up. I remembered a shipyard contact who knew where to procure these specialized materials. With my secret sources, I assembled proprietary repair kits, which Specialty Products then sold regularly to Jackson's company.

In its first nine years, Sirocco had released 38 video programs that focused on doll history, doll artists, doll collecting, and icons in American culture. They established Sirocco as a leading producer of documentary videos and consequently boosted Gayle's and my reputation. In 1997, Gayle and I were honored with the "Who's Who" award from the national Madame Alexander Doll Club for our documentaries on Alexander dolls. We won Telly Awards in the international competition honoring non-network television and non-broadcast video production. Our Telly Award in 1996 was for The Doll Makers; in 1997 for Les Petites Dames de Mode; and in 1998 for Oz: The American Fairyland; in 1999, we also won the Classic Telly Award for the best work in the last 20 years for Hitty, An American Travel Doll; and in 2000 another Telly Award was received for Opulence and Elegance, featuring the events and exhibits of the United Federation of Doll Clubs' 50th Anniversary Convention. Added to this prideful parade were the Videographer Awards honoring special events video productions in 1997 for <u>Doll Art</u>; in 1998 for <u>Oz: The American Fairyland</u>; in 1999 for both <u>Cissy, An American Fashion Legend</u> and <u>Hitty, An American Travel Doll</u>.

Technical Achievement Gold Awards were received for video documentaries in 1999 for <u>Cissy, An Alexander Fashion Legend</u>, for <u>Dewees Cochran, Doll Artist</u>, and for <u>Hitty, An American Travel Doll</u>. In the same year, a Technical Achievement Silver Award for a marketing video was granted for <u>Steel Blasting Systems</u>, one of our industrial videos. Topping everything in 1999 was the Gold Award from Aurora, An International Competition Honoring Excellence in Film and Video Industries, for <u>Cissy, An Alexander Fashion Legend</u>. In the year 1999, Sirocco won eight major, international awards for its documentary videos of which three were for <u>Hitty, An American Travel Doll</u>.

Other hustles, or now that we circulated in an artist crowd, other "inspirations" drifted our way. At the New York Toy Fair in 1997, Paul Crees and Peter Coe, invited us to dinner to explore a business opportunity. Crees and Coe were English designers of theatre costumes, who had turned to designing dolls and had created a buzz among serious collectors with their limited-edition 28-inch-tall Marlene Dietrich doll, produced in poured wax, the traditional English medium. Anne Rice had selected them to produce Lestat, Louis and Claudia dolls, the main characters in her book, <u>Interview with the Vampire</u>. The movie adaptation—with Tom Cruise as Lestat, Brad Pitt as Louis and Kirsten Dunst as Claudia, the deceitful child vampire—added increased marketing momentum. Crees and Coe had the exclusive license to produce these vampire dolls but lacked the operating capital.

Sirocco formed a new corporation, Crees-Coe & Company, with Paul and Peter owning half of the stock, and Sirocco the other half; however, Sirocco retained control as the Managing Partner. With the assignment of the Licensing Agreement from Anne Rice, the new company offered a limited-edition, 28-inch-tall, poured-wax Lestat that was hand painted by Paul and wearing a red-silk cape; and a limited-edition, of 500 pieces of 28-inch vinyl dolls of Lestat and Louis and 18-inch vinyl doll of Claudia. Shipments to fill the special orders from the Anne Rice fans began in July 1998 with the initial orders totaling 40 wax Lestat dolls at a retail price of $1200 each and 101 vinyl Lestats at a retail price of $800 for each doll.

Later, at the United Federation of Doll Clubs Convention in New Orleans in 1999, Anne Rice explained to me why she had selected Paul and Peter. She was impressed with their artistic sensibilities; their prototypes, which brought her characters into the three-dimensional vampires that she had envisioned when writing her book; and their ability to appeal to a larger universe where their artistic creations were perceived as figurative sculptures, not as traditional collector dolls.

As a result of our introduction by Paul and Peter, Sirocco's collaboration with Anne Rice was expanded for our marketing a Perfume and Cologne called the "Lestat Dark Gift" and our distributing the first printing of the first volume in the Sicilian Dragon comic book series, Anne Rice's The Tale of The Body Thief, The Vampire Chronicles in August 1999. Anne Rice autographed all 1000 copies of this first edition.

Adding to the growing relationship was Sirocco's services as the booking agent for John Burbidge, the creator of Les Petites Dames de Mode, costumed mannequins that portrayed a history of Victorian and Edwardian fashions. Sirocco had produced a documentary video on them. Sirocco negotiated a 12-week exhibit of Burbidge's Les Petites Dames de Mode at the new Anne Rice Museum in New Orleans in 1999.

Over the next six years, our Crees-Coe & Company released 13 more limited-edition character dolls in porcelain, including Alexandra, Anastasia, Lucrezia, Fluerette and Savannah; and also marketed other poured-wax dolls, with soft bodies, in limited editions of five or ten pieces. The relationship with Paul and Peter was artistically and economically beneficial.

Addressing a different video market, Sirocco turned out 12 new industrial product videos, averaging 15 minutes in length, primarily for Wheelabrator and its Blastrac equipment and Church and Dwight for its Armex sodium bicarbonate products that were used in cleaning and preparation of wood, aluminum, and stainless steel surfaces.

Producing industrial videos led to another opportunity. Bennie Steele, a Senior Manager of the Paint Department at Newport News Shipyard, asked me to create a Training Program for Deck Coverings and conduct the actual training classes on the installation of specialized

Deck Coverings on military ships. The decks below the flight deck of an aircraft carrier required the installation of unique underlayment products for smoothing and fairing the metal decks; for trowel-applied, joint-less, slip-resistant, fire-retardant terrazzo; ceramic tile in the heads; and a specialized thermoplastic matting to provide a nonconductive surface to prevent electrical grounding through the steel deck, especially important in the radar and radio rooms.

I researched these materials; wrote the training manuals; organized the special tools required for application into proprietary, individual tool kits; hired the experts to teach each specialized class with 15 shipyard employees per class; laid out the class schedules; and supervised the training program in 1999 and 2000 under a Newport News Shipyard contract with Specialty Products. For the hands-on instructors, I hired experienced technicians who would automatically have the respect of the shipyard employees in the class, for example—Channing Walker, known as the Dean of Ceramic Tile Installers in Tidewater Virginia for his work as the foreman for all the tile installation in the Chesapeake Bay Bridge-Tunnel, considered to be the Eighth Wonder of the World; Peter Stoiber, who had helped develop the revised electrical matting specifications; and Tony Alexander, who had 17 years of experience in installing terrazzo decking in ships.

I joked in my introductory lecture to each new shipyard class that I could not use my real name because all the private deck-coating companies had put out a contract for a hit on me. I ended my lecture with "The Navy has provided the platform. Newport News Shipbuilding has provided the opportunity. We have provided the master craftsmen to share their knowledge and experience. You must provide your skills and energy. Together, we can make this a successful opportunity." This teaching program was very successful in Newport News Shipyard's development of its in-house mechanics for installation of these critical coatings on aircraft carriers.

Moreover, Specialty Products continued to supply the unique tools and my proprietary tool kits to the shipyard. Several years later, Tres called my attention to a Purchase Order from the shipyard. "Look at this price," Tres said, pointing to an incorrect price of $38,500 for ten tool kits, when our actual price was $3,850. Since the Purchase Order was already in its system, the shipyard would automatically pay the higher amount. Tres continued: "I've already called the Purchasing Agent and requested an amended Purchase Order at the corrected lower price." I was so proud and thankful that Tres had absorbed my Sassamansville ethics and instinctively had done the right thing.

To market the Sirocco documentary videos directly to our primary audience and to support Gayle's doll business, we attended many regional and national doll collector conventions. Our calendar included events sponsored by the Madame Alexander Doll Club and The United Federation of Doll Clubs, plus the Wizard of Oz, Hitty, Raggedy Ann and Andy, and Doll Art Conventions

Adding the production and marketing of the Sirocco videos, which totaled 57 over a 12-year period, and my industrial teaching activities to my other responsibilities in management and sales at Specialty Products, plus my assisting Gayle at her doll store or at regional doll shows on weekends, made me feel like I was engaged in a Rubik's Cube hustle. Fortunately, the bursts of creative energy and the interaction with doll artists, cultural historians and working authors drove out the remaining psychological clouds from my Swann Enterprise days, balanced the monotonous routine of a small business environment, and were important for maintaining my sanity and generating enough income for economic survival.

But indispensible for my survival was Gayle. We were simpatico from the first moment our eyes met. While I was struggling in my worlds, she was also struggling in her worlds; but we still found time for each other, and together we were greater than the sum of our individual personalities and frenetic energies.

My personal life with Gayle was very pleasant, serene and happy. After 15 years of constant companionship, enjoying each other, and waiting for our children to become independent adults, Gayle and I decided to get married during the Madame Alexander Doll Club Convention in Las Vegas, but we told no one. Our wedding day on July 27, 1996, was memorable. First, Gayle surprised me with a gold tie to wear at the ceremony. It complimented her beautiful ivory dress. When standing in line at the Licensing Clerk's office in Las Vegas, we saw that the Clerk had problems with the couple in front of us; the woman was in her sixties and the man in his early twenties. "Look," the Clerk growled, "your fiancée must be here in person to sign the license, not her mother." At which point, the elderly lady screamed, "Look you putz. I am his fiancée!" Next, the minister at the Riviera Royale Wedding Chapel remarked that it was very sad that we were being married without any family or friends as witnesses. Then we went to our celebratory dinner. Many acquaintances from the Doll Convention stopped at our table, inquired how our day had been and complimented Gayle's beautiful dress and my coordinated gold tie. Suddenly the whole room was laughing and clapping. It turned out that our secret marriage ceremony had been broadcasted live to all the television monitors in the Riviera Casino and Convention Hall.

Gayle moved into Bull Run Court and helped take care of Mother, who had degenerative Parkinson's disease and mild dementia. Practical nurses were on duty with Mother during the days. We installed high locks on the outside doors to keep her from wandering outside.

It was sad to watch the Parkinson's disease invade Mother's body. She would stare at a crossword puzzle in the newspaper. Her eyes confirmed that she had extracted the correct words from her dictionary mind. But she was unable to articulate the words or to write them down. Her eyes then glazed over with her frustration.

With this debilitating and dehumanizing disease, Mother's health was in steady decline and she became bedridden. In mid-February 1998, her doctor diagnosed her life expectancy as a few days. I went to the St. Pius X rectory to summon our parish priest for Last Rites. The priest looked at his calendar and indicated his first available appointment was in three days. I argued with him and literally dragged him to bless Mother.

As Gayle and I held Mother's hands and told her that two of her grandchildren, Heather and Tres, had just learned that they were soon to be parents of baby daughters, Mother opened her eyes for the first time in days. She stared at Gayle and me. We told her how much we loved her and what a wonderful Mother she was. She shut her eyes and stopped breathing. Mother died on February 23, 1998. It was another "saddest day of my life." At the Requiem Mass, I gave the eulogy. I reminisced on Mother's love of words and reading; on her insistence that we always "do the right thing"; and her continuous love that always provided me refuge from the storm. Mother returned to the family mausoleum in Holy Cross Cemetery in Pennsburg to be next to Dad.

A few months later, our Catholic congregation was surprised when the parish priest ran away from his vocation and eloped with a teaching nun from the parochial school. Shortly thereafter, I received a letter from the former priest, who was now a stock broker. "Since I have previously taken care of your spiritual life," he wrote, "I would appreciate the opportunity to meet with you and discuss taking care of your financial life." I sent the letter back with a scrawled note—"I'm sorry but my first open slot is three days after the beginning of never!"

There had been other occasions of shock and sadness. Fred Clarke, the Sales Manager for Specialty Products, raced juiced-up go-carts as a hobby. In a race in May 1992, he had crashed into a retaining wall and was killed in that tragic accident. Frank Freidel had passed away in January 1993, shortly after he sent his laudatory letter on the <u>Dionne Quintuplet Dolls</u> video. Uncle Jack, also suffering from Parkinson's disease, had died in August 1995, removing another connection to Sassamansville. Sassy had expired in 1997, after being viciously attacked by Mother's Siamese cat. I had placed Sassy in a metal doll trunk for her coffin, buried her in the flower garden outside our kitchen window and habitually began each day with "Good Morning, Sassy." Janet Smith, my Administrative Assistant at Swann Oil for over two decades, died in June 1999. I gave the eulogy at her funeral service and applauded her dependability as my trusted friend.

But life, though occasionally sad, continued on. However, it became increasingly focused on our combined family of seven children, 13 grandchildren and multiple relatives, with the never-ending birthday celebrations (April was the busiest month), holidays, school programs, plays, dance recitals, and sporting events. All in all, I was content—particularly with Gayle as the omphalos of my universe. On our anniversary, I gave her an original artist sketch of two Lover's hands with this poem at the bottom —

"This I will remember,
When the rest of life in through;
The finest thing I've ever done
Is simply loving you."

In my quiet, introspective moments, I kept tripping over the phrase, "When the rest of life is through." I had fleeting fears of not living up to my potential and not providing adequately for Gayle and our family. Also, I felt disappointment in myself for not fulfilling Shakespeare's Fifth Age of Man, "the justice . . . with eyes severe . . . full of wise saws."

Drifting Days

There I was, a rehabilitated swan, calm on the surface but underneath, muddling into the millennium, with my mind tuned to beach music one day—"It's the Same Old Song"—and Shakespeare the next—"tomorrow and tomorrow and tomorrow." I was content to have two loyal and loving friends, Gayle and Tres, but there was a subtle concern about mortality as I approached 63, my Dad's age when he died.

Then September 11, 2001, exploded. I remember standing in our comptroller's office, staring at a small television set and watching in horror as the Twin Towers burned and collapsed. The world as we knew it collapsed also. There was the overall feeling of vulnerability from the Middle East terrorists' attacks on civilian targets in the United States and killing some 3,000 innocent people. Perhaps I was more sensitive to that irrational threat because of my first-hand experiences.

The horror of 9/11—just the numbers alone connoted horror—created a flash back to November 22, 1963, the day President John F. Kennedy was assassinated. I remember pulling into a rest stop on the New Jersey turnpike on my way back from the Newark Airport. The restaurant echoed with a low, deadly moaning noise. Women were sobbing. All eyes were on an overhead television set where the news program was replaying the motorcade footage. Multiplying the shock and sadness of November 22 a hundred times would create a perception of the degree of shock and sadness on 9/11. Moreover, 9/11 created another flashback to Sassamansville and memories of how our family and neighbors reacted to the news of December 7, 1941, the bombing of Pearl Harbor.

There was a residual gloom that hovered over our national society and economy. Collectors were less interested in dolls and the sales of Sirocco videos declined dramatically. More Than Playthings, released in 2003, featured artist Wendy Lawton and her hypothesis that dolls were works of art, cultural artifacts and the legacy to connect generations. Sales were disappointing. We decided not to finish the six other video programs that were already shot but awaiting voice-overs and final editing. I now regretted that I had not followed Professor Freidel's advice and switched to national history documentaries like Ken Burns and David McCullough were producing.

Reasons for the decline, besides the gloom of 9/11, were the aging collector base, the lack of interest in dolls as playthings by the younger generation as they turned to computers and electronic gadgets, and the technological advances that replaced the VHS video format with DVDs. Now anyone with a cheap hand-held video camera and a computer could create a video program and duplicate inexpensive DVDs.

Gayle saw the same phenomena affect her doll sales at My Doll House, but even more so, as young girls ignored dolls as passé and became obsessive over the latest computer games. Gayle tried to boost her business by hosting tea parties and birthday parties for young girls, which increased the traffic in the store; but in 2006 when the landlord required higher rent and a 6-year renewal for the lease on her location, she decided to cut her losses and close the store. Hopping aboard the new technology, she would continue her doll business on a very reduced scale by selling on eBay. This was the first time in 42 years, since she was 17 years old, that Gayle did not have full-time employment. It was both sad and exciting for her.

At Specialty Products, demand for the rental of surface preparation equipment and supportive materials became flat as normal maintenance of floors and ship decks seemed less relevant if the nation were facing Armageddon. Business seemed like a slow rocking chair—little motion and no progress.

Tres, who with his innate musical and mechanical abilities reminded me so much of my Dad, initiated adjustments in our business plan. Tres had previously shut down his recording studio but now he organized, with Ira White, Sanctuary Sound as a subsidiary of Specialty Products. Churches suddenly had overflowing congregations at religious services and full collection baskets after 9/11 and were rushing to expand their physical facilities and upgrade their sound systems. Sanctuary Sound would engineer and install the latest sound technology in these churches.

With our in-house fleet of surface preparation equipment and skilled mechanics, the natural evolution was to become a subcontractor to perform the actual floor prep work for the coatings installation contractor. That niche business grew as the established installation contractors could now expand with fewer employees since they had a reliable subcontractor for surface preparation.

At a trade show, Tres discovered a robotic, self-contained blasting system that was designed for the preparation of exterior vertical shells of water storage tanks and petroleum tanks. Specialty Products purchased this unique equipment, which was manufactured in France, and entered another niche market. To understand the technology of coating steel, Tres became a NACE level III Certified Inspector. His credentials led to our first big robotic contract in 2001, for blasting the steel hull of the cutter USS *Resolute* at Baltimore Marine Industries. Next, Tres secured the contract to blast the 32-million-gallon reservoir water tank in Austin, Texas, which was the biggest water tank in the world. With our reputation firmly established by the performance on the Austin tank, and with our other self-contained horizontal equipment for the roof and floor, Specialty Products worked on ground storage and standpipe tanks throughout the United States.

Another surface preparation innovation crossed our radar—the self-contained, rider shotblaster for use on highways and bridge decks to blast off lattices for creating the surface profile for the bonding of new overlayments. This rider shotblaster also removed old, painted line-stripes to prepare for the reinstallation of the new safety lines. Specialty Products purchased propane-engine equipment from Blastrac and later replaced it with 86-horsepower diesel units from B.W. Manufacturing, Inc. We pursued this highway work and won a five-year contract for all the maintenance blasting on highways and bridges for the Eastern District of the Virginia Department of Transportation and also secured work, on a job-by-job basis, in Maryland.

Next, Tres pushed for our becoming the Prime Contractor for the total flooring package—preparation, repair and installation of coatings on the concrete floor. Tres secured his Class A Contractor's License. He went to training schools and qualified our firm as a Certified Installer of Sherwin-Williams General Polymers coatings and floor stains (one of only three in the state of Virginia); Floric Polytech dyes and coatings; and Mapei self-leveling cementitious repair materials for concrete floors.

As Specialty Products evolved into a General Contractor meeting a variety of surface preparation requirements, I was also in front of the parade. I negotiated contracts for the preparation of barge and ship decks—the barges *Columbia* and *Frank DeWitt* and salvage barges USN/YD-245 and USN/YD-255 at Colonna's Shipyard; the vessel USCG *Jupiter* and the salvage ship USNS *Grapple* at Colonna's Shipyard; the *Denobola* in the Staten Island Shipyard; for the flight deck and hangar deck on the aircraft carrier USS *Enterprise* in the Portsmouth Naval Shipyard; the decks and helo pad on the USNS *Fischer* and USNS *Charlton* at Bayonne Dry Dock; and the flight deck on the aircraft carrier USS *George H.W.Bush*, the tenth and final Nimitz Class aircraft carrier to be constructed, in the Northrop Grumman Newport News Shipyard. Plus maintenance work was secured for blasting drydock floors at Colonna's Shipyard and B.A.E. Norshipco Shipyard.

For concrete surface preparation, I was involved in the contract for the repair of traffic lanes on the Annapolis Bay Bridge, which required four large rider-blasting-machines and a crew of 10 operators and laborers on site for three months. Additional projects were the concrete floor repairs for the conversion of a candy manufacturing plant into a computer center in Virginia, the floor preparation at the training center of Consol Energy on the West Virginia line, blasting of concrete walkways at the University of Virginia, floor preparation and leveling at the office building of Metro Machine in Norfolk, and multiple floor repairs and coating projects for Gap, Banana Republic, and Old Navy Store buildouts on the East Coast.

An economic decline in late 2008 occurred from the "Bricks and Slaughter" crisis from subprime mortgages on houses and collateralized debt obligations causing banks to tighten credit, with a resultant negative multiplier effect throughout the entire economy. Specialty Products' business in 2009 declined by 50 percent, and the company suffered its first major nonprofitable year. We scurried to find work. As Morgan Freeman said, "Once you've gotten the job, there's nothing to it. If you're an actor, you're an actor. Doing it is not the hard part. The hard part is getting to do it." I became a persistent bird dog—not a good metaphor for a Swann—looking for any job opportunities.

With the pressures on the contracting business, the surviving General Contractors occasionally became irrational and infrequently were tempted by marginal decisions. A General Contractor hinted to me that he wanted to ignore the CSP-5 protocol for the blasted flooring specifications, to furnish instead a lightly-sanded concrete floor and thus to install less epoxy coating material, which would lower his costs. He reasoned that the Owner would never notice it; and if any wear failure were to occur in the floor coating, it would happen after his warranty period had expired. Offended by his suggestion, I used my Irish diplomacy and responded: "I probably could be tempted to implement your plan if I were to receive $100 million in cash delivered in person by Ingrid Bergman." He replied: "Who is Ingrid Bergman?" Needless to say, our company chose to avoid that project.

Drawing on his mechanical and computer skills, Tres secured an agreement with CeraTech to market its rapid-setting concrete repair materials that could repair airport runways in two hours. Tres qualified Specialty Products for a contract from the General Services Administration as the exclusive supplier of CeraTech products to government facilities and military bases worldwide. Orders flowed from the United States military bases, including those in the Middle East war zone. These sales, with drop shipments from the factory to the end-users, pushed Specialty Products towards its original distribution roots.

Tres also became a Certified Installer of Concrete Dye and Polishing finishes for concrete floors and developed proprietary products for this process. He negotiated an agreement as the exclusive contractor to install this polished flooring system in the new and remodeled West Marine Stores throughout the United States.

Adding Tres' energy and innovations to my energy and persistence, Specialty Products in 2010 had its best year ever. From my office at Virginia Beach Boulevard, which had the same Knoll furniture and Jack Coggins oil paintings for the last two decades, I managed my sales and all of the back office responsibilities with Gail Payne, our comptroller, who had joined us in 1989. I marveled how lucky I was to be experiencing a father-son business dynamic similar to what I had grown up with in Sassamansville. It was exciting to watch Tres exercise his hustle gene.

In my business life, I was competitive, competent and calm; in my personal financial affairs, I was cynically leading a life, as Henry David Thoreau would say "of quiet desperation." It took me 16 years to regain a credit card in my personal name; finally in 2006, I secured a Visa card with a maximum limit of $900. I had no savings and no investments in the Stock Market and therefore was dependent on my share of the profits generated by our business and the company's comprehensive medical insurance for Gayle's and my survival. I felt like a lonely squirrel who could find few nuts to hide even though I knew winter was coming and had to protect my mate.

Once again my understandable senior concerns were prevented from becoming obsessive distractions by the everlasting background chorus from Sassamansville of "There's always a better tomorrow" and "If you rest, you rust"; by Gayle's positive attitude and magnetic energy; by the occasional request for advice from our children; and by invigorating activities with our grandchildren over the decade. I now understood that old rural wisdom—"If I had known that grandchildren were so much fun, I would have skipped the children."

Granddaughters Aubrey and Maggie, on separate trips, accompanied us to New York City, visited the Statute of Liberty, viewed Manhattan from the top of the Empire State Building, roamed the Plaza Hotel where the fictional Eloise had fantasized was her home, and shopped in the exciting F.A.O. Schwartz Toy Store. Granddaughters Hannah, Gabby, Maggie and Aubrey were surprised by a trip to a Swann family reunion at Hershey, Pennsylvania; looked for Willy Wonka as they toured the Hershey Chocolate factory; selected five-pound Hershey bars as their special mementos; enjoyed the candy theme rides at Hershey Park; and explored the mysterious Luray Caverns. Granddaughter Kelsey flew with us to San Diego for a Madame Alexander Doll Convention; made a side trip to see the coastal redwood trees, the largest living trees on our planet, some 350 feet tall and 18 feet in diameter; and skipped across the border to Tijuana, Mexico, to become the first grandchild to visit a foreign country.

I dressed up in my black Stetson, black leather vest, Wrangler jeans and custom-made Lucchese cowboy boots when Grandchildren Kelsey and Ryan accompanied us on the flight to Fort Worth, Texas, for a Madame Alexander Doll Convention. We went to Billy Bob's, the world's largest Honky Tonk, so Kelsey and Ryan—and of course,

Gayle and I—could be photographed riding the bucking bull. There we bumped into a doll salesman, wearing a shoulder bag, the hottest new European fashion for men. As the cowboys around us were tossing their empty beer bottles into strategically placed steel drums, the doll salesman wiggled to the bar for a long-neck bottle of beer and also asked for a glass. "Grab your purse," the bartender bellowed, "and git back to New York City if you need a damn glass!" Kelsey and Ryan saw firsthand that "You don't mess with Texas."

While our social life centered on grandchildren events, my reactions were silently nostalgic and often egocentric. Watching Napoleon Dynamite for our DVD night with the grandchildren, I remembered whining at Hoffmansville School like Napoleon "Whatever I feel like I want to do . . . Gosh!" Enjoying High School Musical on another DVD night, I listened to Zac Efron's "Get'cha, Get'cha, Head in the Game" and drifted back to my High School acting days in Our Miss Brooks. At Grandparents Day at Norfolk Academy, the Headmaster Dennis Manning used the same opening joke every year – "You know that your grandchildren and you share a common enemy – their parents." That had not been the case in my youth as I thought about my hero Dad rescuing me from the wall at Perkiomenville School. At Granddaughter Gabby's talented performance as Honest John in Pinocchio at Norfolk Academy, I slid back to my days as John Alden in One Mad Night and also envisioned Gabby following in Uncle Russell's footsteps to become the next Swann acting on Broadway.

Grandchildren Brad's performance as the Wizard of Oz and Hannah's role as a guard in Emerald City at the Virginia Beach Friends School's production of The Wonderful Wizard of Oz, were well done but I hoped this was my last trip down the yellow brick road. I had seen so many Wizard of Oz school plays and so many versions of Oz during our creation of the video documentary, Oz: The American Fairyland, that the sight of a checkered blue-and-white dress set off a mild panic attack. I had seen so many versions of Toto—from a senior male student, wearing a barrette with floppy dog ears, hopping across the stage on all fours and slobbering like a dog; to a valuable, collectible Beanie Baby dog in a gigantic yellow-straw basket—that I'm positive that Toto was a major contributor to my growing dog phobia.

In an Honor's Ceremony at Oscar Smith Middle School, Grandson Brad missed High Honors because of one grade. I remembered the

B-plus that prevented my graduating Valedictorian at Muhlenberg but refocused on Rachael, four more grandchildren—Morgan, Matthew, Maya and Leah—and what was really important in life. At Grandson Ryan's football games for Oscar Smith High School—he kicked 195 points after touchdowns to hold the Virginia State Record—I stared at the cymbals player in the Marching Band and vibrated back to my banging days as Goose, the percussionist. At Granddaughter Olivia's piano recital, I reminisced about my short stint as a violinist and "Twinkle, Twinkle Little Star." At Granddaughter Aubrey's 16th birthday party, I rambled back to my 16th birthday and my 1946 Ford. At Grandchildren Kelsey's and Ryan's High School Graduation Ceremony with their families cheering and clapping, I heard only the deafening silence at my high school graduation.

The future beckoned as Kelsey began her college career at Virginia Commonwealth University in Richmond, Ryan at Christopher Newport University in Newport News, and Maya at Parsons New School for Design in New York City. Their excitement recreated the rush of my first days at Muhlenberg.

As I watched Grandson Evan, age 4, ride the swing on our backyard gym set, I flew back to the swing that my Dad had hung from the tall tree at our first bungalow in 1941. But this time I had to stay alert for any annoying neighborhood dogs.

A demoniac ghost from the past popped up when Heather called with a major problem in summer 2007. She was 40 years old but her half-brother Paul, as Trustee, refused to turn over her farm trust. The 1979 Trust document provided for the property to be conveyed to Heather at age 35. Paul and his mother were living rent free on the farm. They were operating horse shows under the aegis of the United States Equestrian Federation at the farm and had generated over $4 million of gross revenue during the last 20 years. Nevertheless, Heather's trust had no accumulated income; and not one cent in annual distributions had been paid to her. "I'm afraid to confront Mom about taking over my farm trust," Heather confided to me, "because she has threatened to smash me the way she smashed you in your divorce."

Finally, Heather initiated suit in Montgomery County Court, which unleased a Lebanese tornado counterattack. Four years later and after $220,000 in legal fees, the judge ruled that the 1979 trust be terminated and the deed turned over to Heather, thus making possible the eviction of Paul and his mother. However, under application of the legal concept of laches, Heather was considered to have acquiesced to Paul and his mother's horse shows and their keeping all the show proceeds. They owed her nothing. Another sad outcome was Heather's realization of Paul's minion habit to do anything his mother instructed him to do, including spending his entire adult life, after Harvard and Duke Law School, mucking about the farm and avoiding any professional employment. Heather also experienced her mother's duplicity and vengeful psychopathic personality. It made Heather reexamine the past and reaffirmed that I was not the villain that her mother had portrayed me to be for a quarter of a century. Heather now expended sincere efforts to make up for lost time and strengthen our relationship. She became very close to Gayle and me.

Lost time or the cliché "sands of time" often surfaced in my mind when sunbathing on the beach at Virginia Beach and gazing at the Chesapeake Bay and the Atlantic Ocean. My maritime mind wandered to Captain Christopher Newport and the *Susan Constant*, *Godspeed* and *Discovery* sailing up the James River and settling Jamestown in 1607; to Lord Cornwallis fortunately trapped up the York River at Yorktown in 1781; to the First Battle of Ironclads, the fight between the *Monitor* and the *Merrimac* on March 9, 1862; to the maiden voyage of the *City of Rio de Janeiro*, John Roach's vessel, passing on its way to Rio de Janeiro to begin the United States and Brazil Mail Steamship Company in 1878; to Dad's training at the Norfolk Naval Base and sailing as a radioman on the LST GP-16 for the Pacific theater in 1943; to the tugboat *Maggie Swann* and our barges delivering fresh water and bunker fuel to coal ships anchored in the bay; and to our deck blasting on the aircraft carrier *George H.W. Bush* in preparation for its maiden voyage.

I reminisced about my first meeting with Jennifer and Jackie on the beach, 30 years ago, when I tried to be humorous. "Glad to meet you Jackie," I oozed with a smile. "I didn't know you were Italian." She rolled her eyes and gave an ice-cold reply: "We're Irish, you know."

Or I remembered Katie, Brian Grave's teenage daughter, coming from London to vacation with us. One day we went to the beach. I fell asleep only to be startled awake by a crowd of teenage boys surrounding us. Accustomed to sunbathing on the French Riviera, Katie had removed the top of her bathing suit and was soaking up the sun and stares.

On the roaring waves, I often envisioned the young Ari on his surfboard, a fiberglass Wave Riding Vehicle, propelling majestically toward the beach. Kids laughing in the water caused me to flashback to Olivia and Gabby, at age 5, jumping the waves, again and again—the innocence of youth challenging the eternity of the ocean.

Occasionally I watched the waves and rising tide wash away a sand castle and a sand crab scurry sideways to safety. But often I just stared at the waves and usurped their eternal motion to wash away my concealed depression and to avoid arriving at Matthew Arnold's "Dover Beach." I had lost my entrepreneurial reputation and my financial security; and, for more than two decades, I had to hustle and scurry like an anonymous sand crab just to survive. Other than Gayle and Tres, I had no close friends. I was socially and spiritually isolated, introverted, insignificant and invisible.

Random events, some major and others minor, like the waves and tides, suddenly were triggering moments from the past. I was the "youngest" Swann to marry, to become a father and to divorce. I was the "first" Swann to skip a grade, to graduate from college, to secure advanced degrees from Harvard and to write a book, articles, video scripts and training manuals. I was the "first" and only Swann to file corporate and personal bankruptcy. My history of "youngest" and "first" became a hodgepodge of depressing, unfulfilled potential; of failure in comparison to what my Dad and Uncles Russell, Joe and Jack had achieved; and of monotonous, determined hustles just to survive.

Little in the present created the expectation of swimming from the past into a vibrating future. More frequently, I imagined that I was floating face down in a suspended moment or trapped alone in a sand-crab hole, where only a glance down to the desolation of my past was possible; and a glance up to the future was impossible. It was like being locked in a collapsing sand-crab hole with only downward, fixed-directional telescopic eyes—an indistinguishable, insignificant and isolated sand-crab Swann.

Penultimate Days

There I was, in 2010, after seven decades, in Shakespeare's Sixth Age of Man "with spectacles on nose and pouch on side," trying to remember the nebulous events that made me feel old, alone, lonely, useless and redundant. Perhaps it started with recognizing that my favorite mug read: "I suffer from C-R-S . . . Can't Remember Sh—." It might have erupted when my breakfast was a cold slice of Papa John's pizza and a stale Krispy Kreme doughnut. Maybe it began with my sostenuto dress down from Gucci loafers and Lucchese cowboy boots to SAS tripad comfort shoes. It might have been announced when my rote answer to a waitress' inquiry "How has your day been?" was "Terrible, horrible, no good, very bad day." It might have crystallized when the lyrics "Momma said there'd be days like this, days like this Momma said" became my anthem. Perhaps it struck me when I had two weeks of excruciating pain from kidney stones and scheduled myself for surgery before anyone noticed. Possibly it came into focus when our Granddaughter Hannah, at age 9, gave me a shatter-proof page magnifier. Conceivably, it might have been when our Granddaughter Gabby, at age 11, challenged me to an oxymoron contest; she then pecked away on her Blackberry to win with 57 phrases, while I scratched with a pen on the back of a used envelope with my last two entries—"Sand-crab Swann" and "Intelligent Grandpa." Perhaps it was the parochial parade of other people's preposterous pretensions, physical ailments, pill regimes, proprietary procedures, phenomenal grandchildren and precious dogs.

Ping-ponging from my subconscious were random events. At Gayle's High School Class Reunion, called "A 60th Birthday Party," the class lothario, who flew in from Kentucky, wearing his white Kentucky-colonel hat and Kentucky-Fried-Chicken outfit, and drinking his Kentucky bourbon directly from the bottle, started flirting with Gayle. Instead of my physically popping up to his provocation and propelling myself into the poacher's path, I propositioned Gayle's friend, Lana, with a Benjamin Franklin to knee him in his precious, private parts. "I can't because I just had a knee replacement," Lana replied, "but I will use my other leg and kick him in his 'cannoli' for a Ulysses S. Grant."

Somewhat later, standing in line to buy tickets for one of Grandson Ryan's football games, the senior citizen ahead of me announced to the ticket clerk: "That's Leonard. He stole Gayle, the beautiful flower of South Norfolk. And we're all jealous of him." I could only mutter the stupid retort, "Eat your heart out," as the unknown envier shuffled away.

There was the Christmas Eve dinner at one of Gayle's childhood friends. It was the typical giggle, gabble, gobble, and git-to-church interlude. Sitting across from me was Frances. "Leonard, tell me," she jabbered, "how many pills do you take daily? I take 17." She then proceeded to name every pill and described its size, color and what malady it addressed.

On my right sat a minister's elderly wife. "Leonard," she interrupted me as I was starting to describe my six daily pills to Frances, "I have just had my five-year Colonoscopy; the prep was horrible; the procedure invasive but they gave me a DVD showing every polyp. Modern technology . . . Every polyp."

"That's mighty informative," I mumbled, really thinking T.M.I.—Too Many Idiots—but suddenly realizing why she had that saprophagous grin. "No thank you. I believe I'll pass on the brown turkey gravy."

Next, the dinner conversation took off to bragging about grandchildren. "My granddaughter just made Junior Varsity Cheering and will cheer at all the Junior Varsity Wrestling Matches." . . ."My grandson, he's only 19 months old, said his first words, 'Bucks' and 'Max.' I kid you not. His first words were 'Bucks' and 'Max' for Starbucks and T.J. Maxx." . . ."My grandkid, she's a chip off the old block; she's just graduated from kindergarten." . . ."My youngest grandson's a genius; he discovered sand on the beach." . . ."My granddaughter just switched jobs from McDonald's to Starbucks. Did you know she gets an employee discount on her Double-Tall, Vanilla-Soy Lattes?" . . ."My grandson wants to transfer from Old Dominion University to Virginia Tech. Can you believe that? Become a Hokie!"

At a Birthday Celebration for Granddaughter Olivia in Downingtown, Pennsylvania, hosted by Heather and her husband,

Bob, respectively a veterinary surgeon and veterinarian, while we were waiting for the Birthday Cake, their two miniature schnauzers, Molly and Sparkle, rushed into the room. Molly, the older, licked Sparkle's smeary behind. One of the guests picked up Molly and, as Molly licked her face, oozed "Isn't she sweet? She's so lovable."

"Take a hypothetical situation," I asked with all seriousness, "were your four-year old granddaughter to have just licked feces from her baby sister's bottom, would you pick up the four-year old and allow her to smother you with kisses?" Suddenly, the room became silent. No one talked to me for the rest of the party.

When we arrived back in Norfolk, we surprised our neighbor depositing chicken bones at our front door. She shouted that her dog had crawled in our trash can and dug out the chicken bones, which could choke her dog. I asked her if she could prove the bones were from our trash can. Had she run a DNA test? "Be forewarned," I growled, "I plan to scoop all the dog poop from our lawn, run DNA tests to prove it's from your dog, and deposit it au naturel on your front porch."

She replied superciliously: "You can't take DNA samples from my dog to check for a match without a warrant. I saw it on <u>Law and Order</u>. You need a warrant. And besides, my dog is not accountable because under Bruiser's Law he had no mens rea. I saw it on <u>Legally Blond</u>."

Defeated by the one-two punch of <u>Law and Order</u> and <u>Legally Blond</u> in this kerfuffle, my proclivity for historical analysis kicked in, and I realized that I now could explain why so many men rushed to volunteer for the Confederate and Union Armies during the Civil War. The Southerners enlisted to escape the monotony of grandchildren stories, while the Northerners fled the equally monotonous dog obsessions.

Yet my senescence was only tainted by my sporadic social awkwardness. There was a boring plainness about the aches, annoyances and ambience of growing old, which started with the slight Carpal tunnel pain in my right wrist when I wrote too much; the occasional stinging in my swollen prostate; the shot of pain from a migrating kidney stone; the addition of 40 pounds in the last decade; the indispensable suspenders for my trousers; the awkwardness of bending and putting on my socks and tying my SAS shoes; and the slower gait, labored breathing and rivulets of sweat when I struggled to keep up with Gayle during our exercise walks at the State Park; and ended with my thinning white hair, which now required a number 1.5 head on the electric clipper to achieve the buzz cut that has replaced the flattop of six decades.

The chatter at the old-time Smitty's Barber Shop—with its red and white swirling pole at the front door, porcelain barber chairs and a sign, "Satisfaction guaranteed or your hair back"—no longer concentrated on recent sporting events or the Obama stimulus plan. ("Thirty years ago, we had Ronald Reagan, Bob Hope and Johnny Cash. Today, we have Obama, no hope and no cash.") Now it was medical hour. Every customer and barber talked about his recent surgical procedure, with the most common being bypass surgery for the heart. Who had the latest? Who had the most? The winner was always Marvin, one of the oldest barbers, who pulled up both legs of his pants to show five scars where veins had been removed from his legs for his five heart bypasses.

My barber, J.D., reminded me, during my appointment in late April 2010, that it was the 26th anniversary of his cutting my hair. "Think about it," he said, "26 years of giving you a crew cut every two weeks; and this is the third location of our barber shop. It's remarkable that we're still vertical, ventilating, and venting." Five days later, J.D. had a sudden heart attack and fell over dead. J.D., my barber for 26 years, and I couldn't remember his last name.

Terry, my next barber, lasted for five months before announcing that he was taking a medical leave for surgery to replace both knees. My next barber, John, who was recommended as an expert on buzz cuts, used a fashionable maroon, protective barber drape that showed every gray and white hair. One day, John had a hissy fit when the shop owner insisted that he sweep the mounds of hair from the floor around his barber chair. John grabbed his tools and hopped on the next bus back to New York City. All the barbers, who could give a good buzz cut, were either dying, falling apart or wacky. It was scary since I spent more time in the barber shop than I did in my doctor's office.

During my last annual physical exam, Dr. Keith Sutton, who has been my Internist and one of only two Internists whom I have seen in the last 35 years, had his finger up my butt for the rectal exam and casually commented: "You know that an early sign of Alzheimer's is . . ." Suddenly, I couldn't breathe. What had he found? "An early sign of Alzheimer's is wearing two different colored socks." When I hopped down from the exam table, I glanced down to discover that I was not wearing matched socks—but one blue and the other black.

Other recurring signs of senescence were more subtle. The cashier at Captain D's restaurant automatically deducted the Senior Discount. A 65-year old woman held the door for me at Walmart. Gayle, who everyday for the last 15 years had laid out my coordinated outfit of pants, shirt and sweater-vest, now was including the socks. Mailings from Optima Health urged more frequent preventive screenings for colorectal cancer and prostate cancer. Holloman Brown's Funeral Home bombarded me with brochures on different burial options. Muhlenberg and Harvard sent reminders to include them in my estate planning.

At work at Specialty Products, they have hinted that I was losing it because I was not computer literate or palm pilot efficient. To use a pen was to label myself a dinosaur. Yet, I have worked every business day, talking on the phone to customers, visiting prospective projects, reading blueprints, generating my own proposals, closing sales, negotiating the contracts, reviewing the billing and monitoring the cash flow. As Uncle Joe had pointed out, "You must have a daily routine of showering, shaving, schmoozing and supervising, because, if you rest, you rust." But I was really bored, because as a small, specialized contractor, I was always "Chuck with a Truck" or if lucky, "Chuck with a few Trucks," whereas in the old days I had 700 trucks.

My technological alienation and isolation had increased. Our children, grandchildren, relatives and associates were obsessed with cell phones, computers, palm pilots, e-mail, Facebook, texting and twittering. Our grandchildren suddenly couldn't carry on a coherent conversation at dinner; they were too preoccupied with hiding their hands under the table and pecking away with their thumbs, texting. Even Uncle Dick, in his late 80's, insisted that I contact him only by e-mail to his "Compooter." I had a computer in my office, rarely turned it on, since monitoring and typing my e-mails was a chore for my Administrative Assistant. There were no computers and no blackberries in our house. Sure, I was old school but consider a historical twitter possibility—the length of George Washington's name might have prevented his election as our first President; ponder that John Adams.

It seemed that one criticism hurled at me from all directions was for my collecting hardcover books. "Why do you buy hardbacks when you can borrow the books for free from the library?" . . ."Why purchase hardbacks when you can buy paperbacks for a quarter of the price?" . . ."Why collect hardbacks when you can accumulate your special-interest library on a

'Kindle' or a 'Nook' and carry it everywhere?" ..."Why become a Hoarder, like those eccentrics on that television program, with your clutter of books?" My heritage from Mother's worshiping <u>Webster's Dictionary</u>, my escape in Grade School into the American Classics, my enthrallment with William Shakespeare, my intellectual expansion into history monographs, and my sanctuary between my teeming library shelves—all were manifestations of my benign idiosyncrasy to be analyzed by others. But ink on paper always provided my path of discovery and shield from boredom.

I tried to keep my mental facilities sharp. Each week, I read two to three books—on American History, Shakespeare, True Crime and Business Management. Also on my reading agenda were two daily newspapers—<u>The Virginian Pilot</u> and <u>The Wall Street Journal</u>; three weekly magazines —<u>Time</u>, <u>Newsweek</u>, and <u>The Economist</u>; two monthly magazines—<u>The Atlantic Monthly</u> and <u>Entrepreneur</u>. Plus I skimmed though various publications on business developments and surface preparation. My television addictions included <u>Bones</u>, <u>NCIS</u>, <u>Law and Order</u> and <u>Criminal Minds</u>.

My daily routine was to search for at least one new word and record it in my journal. My recent word list included "Pygmalion Effect" . . . "senescence" . . . "exsanguination" . . . "omphalos" . . . "solipsism" . . ."hemidemisemiquaver" . . . "prosopagnosic." Although at times I worried that by learning new words and forcing them into my conversation was making me weirdly incomprehensible to others. I was becoming an old Jeffy from <u>The Ringer</u> with strange hemidemisemiquavers of thought and bursts of verbal obfuscation.

I kept practicing my alliterations to keep my dictionary mind from fading. For the letter "G," I gushed gaga-gratefully a golden-glow galaxy to describe Gayle as gorgeous, glamorous, genuine, good-hearted, good-natured, gracious, generous, gentle, great, gay, gabby and galoshes galore.

Another activity that helped my sanity, when I was awake at 4AM, was to utilize my degenerative writing skills, not to write history books or documentary video scripts, but to explore other genres and to develop business ideas. (Incidentally, I hold a copyright on everything listed below.) It all started with the annoying bang from the newspaper hitting our front door every morning before dawn. I decided to write an ad for the newspaper —

Delivery Person Wanted.

Strong insomniac to hurl newspaper missiles to explode against front doors, shatter flower pots or disappear in bushes; to abandon newspapers in driveways when raining or snowing; to solicit tips with anonymous holiday cards. Must drive car with roaring engine, rattling muffler and rackety radio.

Then, I began obsessing about a Poetry Reading, à la the Beat Poets, that I had attended at Virginia Beach Friends School's Café Night Fundraiser. Gayle played in an African Drumming Group, comprised of mothers, grandmothers and teachers from Friends School; their African rhythms opened the program. The main event was a self-impressed poet, who was a Virginia Beach version of Willie Nelson but shorter. Dressed in a tie-dyed shirt that was hanging over his beach shorts; sporting a black beret over his long, greying hair; and squinting through round, yellow-framed glasses; he stood up in his flip-flops and recited his "original" poem, entitled "Peace." It called for the end of the evil war in Iraq and peace everywhere. I envisioned my Mother in the audience at "the only rebellion around." I remembered Ted at Harvard and his "Peace, you Mother F—ers." I heard Father Letterhouse muttering that "Old Beatniks never die, they just beat away." Nevertheless, I was challenged to write a poetic retort, pirating the Café-Night poet's key words and parodying his haunting cadence, which I entitled "Oh, Peace!"

Oh, Peace! Where is her "Peace" bling, bling, bling?
It's next to her "Make Peace, Not War" ring, ring, ring.
Why do brave soldiers have to die, die, die?
So she can drink soy lattes in her tie-dye, dye, dye.

Oh, Peace! Where is her "Peace" bling, bling, bling?
It's hanging between her silicon things, things, things.
Why do soldiers in Iraq have to die, die, die?
So terrorists stop blowing silicon rooms high, high, high.

Oh, Peace! Where is her "Peace" bling, bling, bling?
It's stolen to finance a coyote immigrant ring, ring, ring.
Why do American workers pay taxes and cry, cry, cry?
So illegal foreigners can enjoy the American pie, pie, pie.

Oh, Peace! Where is her "Peace" bling, bling, bling?
It's sparkling at a free-trade cling, cling, cling.
Why do self-centered poets spout their jive, jive, jive?
So pseudo-intellects can exchange high five, five, fives.

Oh, Peace! Where is her "Peace" bling, bling, bling?
It's donated to support a "Life is unfair" sing, sing, sing.
Why do idealists embrace injustices and sigh, sigh, sigh?
So naive as populists progress and wave bye, bye, bye.

As I sat alone in my study, sans beret and sans high fives, I thought about my Birthday Party snafu and my chicken bone duel. I began designing "I Hate Dogs" bumper stickers. Picture a logo of a dog squatting on the left side of the sticker and fill in the following slogans on the right.

• I HATE DOGS—ESPECIALLY YOURS
• EVEN TOTO IS ANNOYING
• PAPER or PLASTIC?
• LEASH and ORDER
• YOUR ANTHROPOMORPHIC DOG IS STUPID . . . TOO
• BEND and SCOOP
• WHO'S the DUMB ONE HERE?
• A.V.O.I.D. —ADULTS VERY OPPOSED to IDIOT'S DOGS
• GOT METHANE?
• NO BITCHES on BEACHES
• HAVE YOU SCOOPED TODAY?
• CANINEOREXIA—the OTHER OOGEDY-BOOGEDY

I have written dozens more but that's enough of this dogged picture. Interestingly, my Insurance Broker refused to write liability insurance for Sirocco to produce these stickers because she was afraid that dog lovers would key scratch any car displaying anti-dog bumper stickers. Then one day, I bumped into her at the beach, walking her German Shepherd! Shortly thereafter, I awoke from a nightmare, where Gayle and I were attending a performance at the Wells Theatre in Norfolk. The lead actress walked on stage with two German Shepherds, one named "Villanova" and the other, "Virginia Beach." They stopped suddenly, their hackles bristling, pointed into the audience and started barking furiously. The German Shepherds leaped off the stage into the startled audience and attacked me. I couldn't get back to sleep, because humming in my mind was the pop tune—"Who let the dogs out? Who? Who?"

My second topic was a more benign series of bumper stickers for the grandmothers with their boring grandchildren stories. Called the McBooger series, picture Detective McBooger, a cartoon character like Lieutenant Columbo, who is picking his big nose, positioned on the left side, and the slogans on the right, for example:

• McBOOGER'S ALWAYS HANGING OUT
• McBOOGER'S GOT HIS HEAD IN THE GAME
• McBOOGER GETS TO THE ROOT OF THE PROBLEM
• McBOOGER, WHERE ARE YOU HIDING?
• McBOOGER, COME OUT, COME OUT WHEREVER YOU ARE
• McBOOGER'S IN THE HOUSE
• McBOOGER, A FRIEND IN TIGHT PLACES
• MeBOOGER: PARTING IS SUCH SWEET SORROW
• McBOOGER: TO SNOT OR NOT TO SNOT,
            THAT IS THE QUESTION
• HOOK 'UM UP, McBOOGER
• BOOK 'UM, McBOOGER

There were dozens more and even plans for a children's illustrated book with Detective McBooger as the hero. Picture full-page drawings, each with a single line: "So you think you're being picked on" . . ."It runs in the family" . . ."I never met a McBooger that I didn't like" . . ."If you've got it, flaunt it." Or patriot McBooger, wearing a tricornered colonial hat, with the declaration—"Give me Liberty or Give me Snot" . . ."The snot heard around the world" . . ."How's that Hopey-Boogey thing workin' out for ya now?" But enough McBooger.

My next secret graphomania project was to write a musical comedy on women's shopping. This idea was inspired by my lovely Gayle, who shoe shops frequently and is closing in on Imelda Marcos. Or perhaps Gayle, like Cinderella, is trying to save me, one Ugg at a time. The female lead tap dances onto the stage and sings:

> "I'm so excited. I just can't hide it.
> Marshalls has Michael Kors' shoes,
> With the bronze peace buckle astride it.
> I'm so excited. I'm so excited."

In slouches the male lead, carrying a solitary Kors' box, and delivers his blues solo:

> "I've got the 'What's wrong with this story' blues,
> My wife's a determined shopping fox,
> Who's searched and searched for Michael Kors' shoes,
> Then rewarded me with the Kors' cardboard box.
> I've got the 'What's wrong with this story' blues."

In Act II, the female performer, dazzling in sparkling gold-sequined boots, swirls across the stage.

> "I'm so excited. I just can't hide it.
> V.P. Shoes is discounting Uggs, Uggs, Uggs,
> Gold boots with sequins for hugs, hugs, hugs.
> I'm so excited. I'm so excited."

Her male counterpart struggles on stage, balancing a tall pyramid of Ugg boxes, and lets loose his finale in the key of C.

> "I've got the 'What's wrong with this story' blues.
> My wife's switched from Kors to Uggs, Uggs, Uggs,
> She's now buying boots in addition to shoes,
> And hands me more boxes and shrugs, shrugs, shrugs.
> I've got the 'What's wrong with this story' blues."

The pyramid of Ugg boxes crashes as the curtain falls. When the audience exits through the lobby, they hear a recording of Ralph Stanley singing his bluegrass classic, "I'm breaking in my new pair of shoes."

Another diversion was writing jokes, perhaps for a comedian like Carlos Mancia, or George Lopez, such as:

- What happens when you mix a Burrito with Irish Whiskey?
  - You get a Chimichanga singing "Ole' Danny Muchacho."

- . . . a Burrito with Irish stew?
  - a Chimichanga in green leotards.

- . . . a Burrito with a Starbucks Grande Vanilla-Soy Latte?
  - a bankrupt Chimichanga.

- . . . a Burrito with French Fries?
  - a Chimichanga that runs backwards.

- . . . a Burrito with guacamole on St. Patrick's Day?
  - a Chimichanga singing like Tony Bennett, "What's up Leprechaun?"

My fear of developing Alzheimer's led to another series of jokes for delivery by a Blue Collar comedian, perhaps Jeff Foxworthy, for example: You might have Alzheimer's . . .

- . . . if Jeffery Dalmer asks if you want white or dark meat and you answer "Whatever."
- . . . if you call AAA for emergency service on your power scooter.
- . . . if you take a soup spoon and begin eating from the Key Bowl.
- . . . if you grab the TV remote control, push 911 and keep asking: "Can you hear me now? Can you hear me now?"
- . . . if you point a pen at a bank teller and yell, "Give me all the money or I'll shoot you!"
- . . . if you are running butt-naked down the street and yelling, "A towel, a towel, my kingdom for a towel."
- . . . if you are skipping down the double yellow lines in the middle of the highway and singing, "Follow the yellow-brick road."
- . . . if you wake up every morning with a different woman.

• . . . if you transfer from Old Dominion University to Virginia Tech.

But underneath my façade of frivolity was a loneliness, an emptiness, a desperation, a mental exsanguination that only someone who has been there can relate to with any empathy. I had an overriding sense of being a nobody, a failure, an unaccomplished, unappreciated, unrewarded and unrecognized nobody, where only the sounds and smells of senility proved that I still existed.

The smell of decay and impending death had been creeping up everywhere. Consider the events of the week before a recent birthday:

• We rented a "must see" movie, <u>The Savages</u>. Its plot centered on an aging-senile father named "LEONARD" and the efforts of one of his kids to stash him away in an old age home.

• Just two days after our last meeting, a long-time customer from Ocean City, Maryland, phoned me and started his conversation: "Leonard, my man, do you remember me?"

• A front page article in <u>The Wall Street Journal</u> reported: "Everyone is 'Cane Fu' fighting at Senior Center, so watch out." A new trend of cane fighting started at St. LEONARD'S Retirement Center in Centerville, Ohio, where Bingo was replaced by Martial Arts Cane Fighting.

• A magazine article reported that the most important investment for aging Baby Boomers is a "walk-in shower." Guess what my birthday present was? Jennifer and Jackie repainted my bathroom and fixed-up my walk-in shower.

• Another long-time customer, age 58, in North Carolina died suddenly and painfully of a massive brain tumor.

Any death of an acquaintance automatically released some subliminal sadness lingering from the loss of my Dad and Mother. In fact, I thought about them every day. My habit of stacking the dishwasher the way my Mother had taught me—with the dirty dishes descending in size from the back to the front—was a daily trigger for sadness. Scrolling through my fond memories and lighting votive candles before Mass did not dispel the enveloping sadness and loneliness.

The sights and smells of loneliness were everywhere, sometimes stronger than others. Last October, I drove alone for ten hours to attend the wedding of Alexandra Stevenson, my second cousin and the granddaughter of Uncle Dick, my last living uncle. It was held at an isolated vineyard at Mount Airy, Maryland. Uncle Dick, in his wheelchair, gave a blessing at the ceremony. I recognized only nine people at the wedding, a realization that reinforced my loneliness. As I left the reception, a Hank Williams song, "I'm so Lonesome I Could Cry," which my Dad always played on his guitar and sang, was pouring from my car radio: "Did you ever see a robin weep, when leaves begin to die? Like me, he's lost the will to live. I'm so lonesome I could cry." I fantasized that I was going to the Hickory Park stage to see my Dad perform in person. At that moment I came down a hill, drove past a lake, and saw one lonely swan swimming. No one can imagine how lonely and vulnerable I felt. Why? Was it really the fear of dying?

Another family event raised the same apprehension. On January 16, 2011, there was a ceremony at St. Joseph Roman Catholic Church, Odenton, Maryland, for the retirement of Uncle Dick after 25 years of faithful service as a Deacon. At the reception, the crowd gathered around Uncle Dick, age 89, in his wheelchair, included a cousin who was limping because her knee replacement surgery was on hold; another relative who was recovering from a heart attack; and still another with a breathing tube and portable oxygen tank, who announced that he was waiting for the emergency call from the hospital to tell him that his matching lung donor had died and his replacement surgery was scheduled. All three were younger than I. That gathering was depressing and also raised the spiritual question, should a Catholic pray for a matching donor to have an accident and subsequently die in order to harvest his body parts so that the petitioner could continue living? There was no Father Letterhouse to consult.

If I defined myself as depressed, diminished and deserted as opposed to vital, viral and vigorous, would it be better to cease living? If I categorized myself as a defeated man, an insignificant man, an invisible man, would it be better to cease living? I found myself praying over and over again for a fatal heart attack in my sleep. I rationalized my prayers for a fatal heart attack in my imaginary conversation with Dad at the Hickory Park creek: "Yes, Dad, I can then skip the clever alliterations and tell you face-to-face all the good things that have happened since last we spoke in person on August 2, 1981." But was praying for a fatal heart attack the same as assisted suicide and thus a mortal sin? There was no Father Letterhouse to consult.

I would not seek spiritual guidance from the pip-squeak priests at St. Piux X parish in Norfolk. My previous experience with a local priest, who was dilatory in coming to give Last Rites to my Mother as she lay dying, left a spiritual void, which was not as cataclysmic as the experience that Anne Rice recounted in her book, <u>Called Out Of Darkness</u>, but mine was a very negative experience, nevertheless. Over the recent years, I had discovered that a perverted priest from a Virginia Beach church had been transferred to continue his ministries at a rural parish on the Eastern Shore of Virginia. I had witnessed an effeminate priest continuously playing with his cassock sleeves throughout mass, even during the Blessing of the Eucharist. I had encountered our two parish priests drinking, eating and laughing at El Azteca, a Mexican Restaurant, while many of their parishioners were on their knees at the Easter Eve prayer vigil; and at a 2010 Christmas Mass, I had listened to our new, really-short Filipino priest, as he stood on a wooden box behind the lectern, and sang a cappela the entire John Lennon's song "Happy Christmas" instead of delivering a joyous Christmas sermon—"So this is Christmas and what have you done? Another year over, a new one just begun." There was no Father Letterhouse to consult.

Nor would I visit a psychiatrist. My first experience with that profession had involved an interview and testing, in 1959, to prepare a "Vocational Guidance Report" for my file at Harvard—fortunately for me after I had been accepted at Harvard. "It would be very helpful," the psychiatrist observed, "for Mr. Swann to develop his insight and understanding of people and their motives . . . he can become rather critical and negative in his outlook." My next memorable experience was after Dad died. "You are a wimp," the genius psychiatrist concluded, "for sublimating your fears and not leaving immediately after burying your Dad." My final experience with psychiatric interviewing was a court—mandated visit, as part of my divorce proceedings in the mid-1980's, where I discussed my potty training in a yellow and brown tirade. There was no Father Letterhouse to consult.

So I turned to hardbacks in my study for answers and guidance. William Shakespeare was some help. "I have not the alacrity or spirit, nor cheer of mind, that I was want to have," as he wrote in <u>Richard III</u>, described my mood. But Hamlet's musing on "the undiscovered country from whose bourn no traveler returns" or the King of France's declaration in <u>All's Well That Ends Well</u>, "Let me not live after my flame lacks oil" were discouraging. Shakespeare in <u>As You Like It</u> was totally discouraging, starting with Touchstone's observation, "And so from hour to hour, we ripe and ripe, and then from hour to hour, we rot and rot, and thereby hangs a tale." Then Jaques lists the Seven Ages of Man, with senility, the last age, reduced to "second childishness and mere oblivion, sans teeth, sans eyes, sans taste, sans everything."

"It was a shame," wrote Dennis Cattrell in <u>The Law of Gravity</u>, "that everything you'd felt and heard and thought and went through didn't matter to other folks." My sentiment exactly, more so when I envisioned myself described by John Updike as "white haired and wed to aging loneliness." But then I tripped over a psychological bomb from Thomas Hood, who wrote in the early 19th century: "When he is forsaken, withered and shaken, what can an old man do but die?" And Herman Melville added in <u>Moby Dick</u>: "Where lies the final harbor, whence we unmoor no more?"

There were undercurrents of psychological disconnection and a disappointment in myself, an existential embarrassment of failure and a fear of dying with failure as my legacy. I had no interest in bonding with an anthropomorphized pet or searching for e-mail phantoms on a computer as chatting buddies to buffer my loneliness and to boost my diminishing spirits. I was alone and lonely. I had only myself with my weakening eyes, my waxing ears, my wandering mind and my waning energy as the withering bulwarks for my weaving sanity as I awaited my swan song.

I kept hearing in my mind the voice of Leroy "Satchel" Paige, the oldest rookie in the Major Leagues as a pitcher for the Cleveland Indians. Satchel kept saying: "Age is a case of mind over matter. If you don't mind, it don't matter." But I did mind. And it did matter, because I knew that I was no longer what I was.

Believe it or not, it was a song by Kathy Lee Gifford that nudged my partial return from this god-awful funk and pushed me toward a resigned, somewhat bearable loneliness—"I don't want to be aggravated, agitated, obligated, exasperated, underrated, manipulated, intimidated, deprecated, dominated, dilapidated, denigrated, constipated . . . I just want to be the old me." That was it! I just wanted to be the old me! I just wanted to be the old me!

Gayle, my faithful companion and friend for over three decades, provided a loving and stabilizing energy. In our peaceful home, she radiated positive energy and urged me to think positively to attract positive karma. She gave me <u>The Secret</u> by Rhonda Byrne, which introduced me to the Law of Attraction—"like attracts like" . . ."when you feel good, you are powerfully attracting good things to you." She hung a sign on my study door—"Some People Pursue Happiness; Others Create It." Gayle planned fun moments, quality time, including day trips to Colonial Williamsburg, lunch at Christiana Campbell's Tavern, and rummaging at Mermaid Books; and to Ocean City, Maryland, for a scrumptious Crab Cake lunch at the Crab Cake Factory, shopping for grandkids' clothes at Coconut Kids, searching for old Shakespeare books at the Antique Bookstore, and finding the latest Ugg boots at V.P. Shoes. Another memorable excursion was to the Virginia Museum of Fine Arts in Richmond for the traveling exhibit of 176 Pablo Picasso masterpieces from the Museé National Picasso, Paris and then to Black Swan books, the out-of-print bookstore. But I noticed that important planning considerations for each itinerary and travel route were the locations for Starbucks coffee breaks, familiar rest stops for bathroom breaks, favorite restaurants for the rigid mealtimes; and collector bookstores for out-of-print and rare books.

All in all, Gayle tried very hard to make my world emotionally complete, with frequent mindful gestures, such as leaving a card quoting Robert Browning on my desk —

"Grow old along with me!
The Best is yet to be,
The last of life, for which the first was made."

Daughter Deborah, a successful attorney and no longer called "Debra" or "Debby," sent me a letter for Father's Day: "I remember sitting on the handle bars of your black bicycle as you rode me to the Leslie-Ellis School. I remember Rachael with her Harvard frog, your song about 'John Roachie, John Roachie' while you were writing your book and my sitting at your desk practicing the alphabet to get ready for the first grade—trying to write the alphabet but basically just drawing pictures. Oh such a long time ago! And so many more memories that follow. All very good; all a pleasure to think about."

Jennifer and Jackie, our daughters, sent me notes. Jennifer wrote: "My hope is that through your gracious giving, I will learn to be a selfless giver." I was thankful for how kind they had been to me over the years and genuinely proud of how they had succeeded as graduates from Old Dominion University and how well they had matured as responsible mothers. They set the standard for their brother Ari's parenting of his son Kai.

Grandpa geezer moments came from Kai, our youngest grandchild. Gayle babysat Kai at our house during the week—what an active, happy little boy, just shy of two years old. For Christmas, I spent two whole days, with a screwdriver as my buddy, and a Chinese drawing as my road map, assembling 260 wooden pieces into a train table with track layout and a village, which reminded me of Sassamansville. I had never before in my entire life devoted two days to assembling a toy. It was frustrating because the pieces of track curved in the opposite direction and would not fit together. Then a piece fell on the floor; and I discovered that there were track grooves on both sides of all the curves and the piece could be turned over to match the curve of the track pattern. That falling piece of track changed my classification of Chinese engineers, who I remembered ate bologna, from stupid to intelligent but raised the reciprocal concern about why it had taken me so long to find the solution.

Kai loved playing with wooden trains on his train table. Then Kai started quoting me and only me. When his parents were jumping up and down at the dinner table, Kai remarked "Leonard says 'Sit'!" When his Dad called him for his bath, Kai replied "Leonard says 'No way, Jose'!" And when his parents would be upset with his mess of toys on the floor, Kia declared "Leonard says 'Enough Already'!" Kai's most favorite toys were his hard hat and measuring wheel, which I had given him so that he could help me survey potential job sites. Kai carried his measuring wheel everywhere.

And there were other positive moments cropping up. Our Granddaughter Gabby had a writing assignment for her English class at Norfolk Academy—to interview her favorite relative on something missed from childhood and the happiest childhood memory. Gabby chose me and reported on my emotional reminiscing about the family music sessions, over 60 years ago, in my parents' basement. As I told Gabby, when I think back to those happy family gatherings, I realize how the Sunday music sessions provided a sense of security, a built-in monitor of a positive value system, a pulsating example for instinctively doing the right thing, of helping each other, of sharing with each other—in effect, a simple confirmation of our essential humanity. Today, with families spread out to distant places and computer communications, we are isolated in an impersonal world where the comfort of family, the goodness of family and the joy of family have been diminished. So I miss those Sunday jam sessions and my Dad's voice—"Jack, Jack, we're playing this one in the key of C."

Out of the blue, Daughter Heather suddenly announced that she wanted to move her family from Downingtown to Norfolk, because she felt very happy when in the company of Gayle and me. She began actively looking at houses for sale that were close to Bull Run Court and reviewing private schools for Olivia.

Then on Valentine's Day in 2011 —Yes, Valentine's Day—I was in the attic and stumbled across two of my Mother's cedar chests and a half-dozen boxes that had been stacked there since 1986, when Mother had moved to Norfolk to live with me. In them, I found hundreds of photographs of virtually every Swann and Brey relative and most major family events—including snapshots of my parents' early years together; dozens of school photos of David and me; photos of Dad and my Uncles wearing their World War II uniforms; plus other photos of company trucks and business facilities. My report cards from grade school through high school; three <u>Wallum Olum</u> yearbooks from my high school years; three <u>Ciarla</u> yearbooks from my Muhlenberg years; a plastic garment bag, labeled with my name, that contained my blue baby bunting; an old gift box with my Boy Scout shirt, complete with "Order of the Arrow" insignia, and my sash with all my merit badges; tickets for admission and programs from my graduations from Upper Perkiomen, Muhlenberg and Harvard. Some boxes contained thousands of yellowed newspaper clippings—obituaries of Father Letterhouse and many of our Sassamansville neighbors; articles about my uncles; articles written about me or by me; articles on our petroleum business; pristine copies of magazines with articles on the Swann business ventures and magazines I had published in Virginia, North Carolina and

South Carolina. Included in one box were my underlined script books for <u>One Mad Night</u> and <u>Our Miss Brooks</u> and programs, theater tickets and photos taken at play practice. There was even the "Regulations" booklet on the United States Naval Academy in the original envelope from Senator James Duff. Letters from Mother's family, grandchildren and friends—even some carbon copies of typed letters that she had written to me at Harvard. The list could go on and on, but suffice to say, there was enough original source material for a history of our family. This treasure trove of information was a historian's dream.

As I foraged through those musty treasure chests, opened the rusty tabs on old manila envelopes, and peeked into yellowing file folders labeled with my Mother's faded handwriting, I teared up and finally broke down crying. The answers were all here for the who, what, where and why of my being. It didn't matter that I was old and in the words of e.e.cummings, "have known autumn too long." It didn't matter that I had contributed so little to posterity since I was not a teacher, not a writer, not a preacher, not an inventor, not an entrepreneur and not a healer. It didn't matter that I sat alone in my study to read, jot, clip, file and stress about the inevitable Shakespeare's Seventh Age of Man—"second childishness and mere oblivion." What mattered was that my Mother loved me, then and forever. What mattered was that my Mother was reminding me that I was a Swann and a country boy. What mattered was that my Mother was calling me back to be the old me—not to be demeaned or diminished or dismissed—but simply to be the old me. What mattered was that my Mother was telling me to share my story.

Apple Butter Day

There I was, in spring 2011, sitting alone in my study at Bull Run Court, flanked by shelves of books. My collection of more than 5000 hardbacks includes monographs of American History, Naval and Maritime History, Economic Theory, critical studies of William Shakespeare's works, Doll Collecting encyclopedias, and True Crime documentaries. Plus there are copies of <u>John Roach: Maritime Entrepreneur</u> and all the Sirocco videos.

Scattered about are Harry Bertoia bronze sculptures, a replica of the USS *Constitution* in a glass bottle, a vintage Harvard lamp, a baseball autographed by the starting lineup of the 1980's Championship Philadelphia Phillies, a framed two-faced nickel from Uncle Russell's magic props, a hand-carved Hitty, and small sculptures of William Shakespeare, St. Francis of Assisi and a green squatting Buddha with a female head. On the file cabinet are a blue baby bunting, an old tiger blanket and a gift box with a gold tie.

On top of my video-editing monitor are chotskies from my youngest granddaughters—a Happy Feet penguin from Gabby, a paper-mache swan created by Maggie, a woven-paper bow fashioned by Aubrey, a large eraser with a decal of a Benjamin Franklin bill from Hannah, and a wooden cat, hand-carved and painted by Olivia.

Featured on the walls are antique oil paintings of sailing ships and an early steam tugboat. There are also watercolor and oil paintings of sailing vessels by Jack Coggins; two floral paintings by Alma Coggins; antique lithographs of the City of Philadelphia and John Roach's shipyard in Chester; portraits of John Roach, William Shakespeare and St. Iofunudi; and oil paintings of Hoffmansville School and two swans swimming in a lake; a framed crayon-drawing of a cat, made by daughter Heather at age 6, which reads "To Dad, Love Heather," and a colored photo of Sassy.

Also displayed are a framed copy of Judith Viorst's book, <u>Alexander and the Terrible, Horrible, No Good, Very Bad Day</u>, and painted wooden signs stating "The 13th Commandment—Thou shall not be a Smart Ass" and "Irish Diplomacy—the ability to tell someone to go to hell so that he will look forward to the trip."

Multiple framed photographs hanging on the walls include my Grandpa and Grandma Swann, celebrating their 50th Wedding Anniversary, sitting in rocking chairs on the front porch of their farm house; collages of Mother and Dad; shots of Gayle's Mother and Father; pictures of Tres, including him in the wheelhouse of the *Evgenia K. Chimples*; and an array of Gayle, as a young girl holding a baby doll, as a champion fisherwoman with a trophy blue marlin and a series of studio portraits of Gayle, covering our extremely happy decades together; and charming snapshots of various grandchildren.

As I daydream at my Knoll oval desk that had passed down from my Dad, flanked by my Mother's antique cedar chests and a stack of Ugg boxes, surrounded by my 72 years of collected books and detritus of objective correlatives that define my world, my eyes inevitably focus on a mundane item positioned on a bookshelf—a 19-ounce glass jar with the label "Bauman's Pennsylvania Dutch Apple Butter . . . Sassamansville, Pa."

Staring at that Apple Butter jar transports me back into another time and place. The letters in the words "Apple Butter" reveal the anagram of the geographic and cultural influences during the formative period of my life. The geographic boundaries are defined by the letters, "A" . . . "P" . . . "P" . . . "R" for Allentown, Pennsburg, Pottstown and Reading, with the tiny village of Sassamansville squatting in the middle of the eastern perimeter. Each letter reveals the elements of a value system that was integral, influential and indispensable to my survival for more than seven decades, specifically —

A	Analyze each situation, because sometimes it's better to sit on the porch, drink a Coke and lose a little money than to work hard in the field and lose a lot of money.
P	Push yourself, because Grandma taught "you can do anything you want to do."

P . . . .   "Positive thoughts and proactive hustles produce positive results" summarized Dad's plan.

L . . . .   Look in your Mother's antique cedar chests for the who, what, where and why of your existence.

E . . . .   "Every person is very special" was key to Grandpa's philosophy of life, because he added, "if everyone thought the same way, they would have married your Grandma."

B . . . .   Be active because, as Uncle Joe warned, "If you rest, you rust."

U . . . .   "Unless you're blind," as Uncle Jack declared, "you can always tell when a banker or lawyer is lying—it's when his lips are moving."

T . . . .   "This above all: to thine own self be true, and it must follow, as the night the day" was the wisdom shared by William Shakespeare.

T . . .   "There is always a better tomorrow," as Grandma promised again and again on her back porch.

E . . . .   Eucharistic Faith in the Catholic religion, practicing it and always doing the right thing, as Father Letterhouse preached at Grandpa's Requiem Mass, will guarantee that "The world will mourn over the loss of a good man, but heaven will rejoice over the gain of a saint."

R . . . .   "Remember," as Dad wisely counseled, "never let the bastards get you down and never, never let the S.O.B's know that you're hurting."

From the epicenter of that Apple Butter jar emerges a little boy, called Sonny, walking down the road in the tiny village of Sassamansville. Mother and Dad are coming toward him. They are smiling and greet him—"We are proud of you for remembering who you are . . . . Welcome Home . . . . Son of Sassamansville."

Acknowledgements

There I was, staring at my book cases, not really believing that I had captured my memory and finished scribbling.

I must begin by thanking my Mother for her compulsive saving of the paper and photographic detritus of our life, then bringing it with her to Norfolk and archiving it in our attic. She supplied the documentary treasure trove for the early years. And apparently I inherited her habit of collecting and filing, which was helpful for tracing the later years. Thank you, Mother.

I want to thank Gayle for encouraging me to write this memoir and for tolerating the long hours that I spent in my study during the three consecutive months of "rememberin', researchin' and 'ritin'." Her proofreading and editorial comments plus searching through photographs were indispensible. But most of all, I want to thank her for the loving security, positive balance and aura of completeness that she has brought into my life.

Next, I want to thank Tres for covering for me in our business. Even though I was physically in the office during normal business hours, my mind was often elsewhere as I jotted down remembrances on my note cards or edited the computer drafts. I am in awe and thankful for his computer skills in assembling the photographs in "Picture Days." And I am most thankful for his participation in replicating the wonderful Father-Son relationship that was and continues to be a keystone in my life. For that, I also must thank my Dad, my idol forever.

I am very appreciative for Denice Moran, my Administrative Assistant, for her patience and skill in translating my messy cursive writing into a computer format. I am especially thankful for her hidden artistic talents that she revealed when she volunteered to design the dust jacket.

I thank Ari for using his skills to shoot the photograph for the dust jacket and other current photos in my memoir.

And finally, I must acknowledge Kai who just popped into my study with his measuring wheel and instructed me—"Enough Already!"

Leonard A. Swann, Jr., a graduate of Muhlenberg College and Harvard University, is the author of <u>John Roach, Maritime Entrepreneur,</u> numerous magazine articles, and 40 scripts for documentary videos in the Sirocco Historical Doll Series and the Sirocco Master Artist Series. He currently resides in Norfolk, Virginia, with his wife and surrounded by 7 married children and 15 grandchildren. Once again, Kai is declaring "Enough Already!"